INTRODUCTION

Technology gets more and more complicated in an effort to provide more and better goods at a lower cost. New technology provides impressive levels of productivity but requires very high investments. New technology is usually very expensive and very complicated — particularly for the home experimenter.

The backyard mechanic on the other hand is not interested in productivity. If in operating his backyard foundry, he makes one casting an afternoon and enjoys what he's doing, then he does not need the new high-priced technology. Old methods will do.

The purpose of this book is to preserve old methods before they become lost forever.

Blacksmithing is not so much making horseshoes, hinges and sharpening plowshares, as it is a general method of working iron where complicated machines are replaced with simple tools and the skill gained from a long apprenticeship.

"Iron Forging" won't teach you all the skills that an expert blacksmith could, but you *will* learn skills that are usually not covered in other blacksmithing books. Since this is a reprint of a book published at the turn of the century when blacksmithing was still very much alive, you can be sure that what you read here is genuine and useful.

Read and enjoy.

WARNING

Remember that the materials and methods described here are from another era. Workers were less safety conscious then, and some methods may be downright dangerous. Be careful! Use good solid judgement in your work. Lindsay Publications has not tested these methods and materials and does not endorse them. Our job is merely to pass along to you information from another era. Safety is your responsibility.

Write for a catalog of other unusual books available from:

Lindsay Publications
PO Box 12
Bradley IL 60915-0012

Blacksmith Shop & Iron Forging

"Lost Technology Series"
reprinted by Lindsay Publications

Blacksmith Shop &
IRON FORGING

reprinted from a volume published in 1906 by
International Correspondence Schools

ISBN 0-917914-07-4

5 6 7 8 9 0

BLACKSMITH-SHOP EQUIPMENT

HEATING DEVICES

FORGES

STATIONARY FORGES

1. Brick Forge.—A **forge** is an open fireplace, or hearth, with forced draft, arranged for heating iron, steel, and other materials. A very serviceable form of **brick forge** is shown in Fig. 1. The hearth is usually rectangular in shape, and 26 or 28 inches in height. For ordinary work, the front *a b* may be from $2\frac{1}{2}$ to 3 feet long, and the side *b c* from 3 to 4 feet long. An iron water trough 6 to 8 inches wide is often fastened along the side *b c*. The brickwork is usually built with a space *f* in the top, for the fire and fuel. The depth of this space varies greatly, according to the work and the ideas of the workman, but it is usually from 4 to 8 inches; the bottom consists either of brickwork or of an iron plate, supported on bars.

The forge is usually provided with a hood to catch the smoke and lead it into the stack or chimney; Fig. 1 shows a sheet-iron conical hood attached to the chimney, but the hood may be square and is sometimes built of brick.

Where there is plenty of room in the smith shop and the blast is supplied by hand power, the brick forge is the type most frequently used. The advantages claimed for it are that it is little affected by the moisture of the atmosphere, costs less for repairs than the iron forge, and the form of the hearth may be quickly and easily changed to suit the requirements of the various classes of work.

2. Forge Tuyères.—The bottom of the forge shown in Fig. 1 has a suitable opening cut in it, in which is fitted a **tuyère iron** (pronounced *tweer* iron), sometimes called an **air chamber,** or a **wind box,** for the purpose of admitting air under the fire. The bottom of the tuyère iron has an opening about the same size as the opening cut in the

Fig. 1

bottom of the forge. This opening is closed by a valve of thin sheet iron by means of the handle *s*.

In Fig. 2 is shown a section of one form of tuyère iron commonly used. It has an opening *j* in one side, and one *g* in its top. The side opening is connected with a pipe through which air is supplied to the fire. The top opening is usually capped with a nozzle *b*, and fitted with a valve *c*. This valve is made so that it will admit air to the fire and permit the cinders to drop into the bottom *e* of the tuyère iron. Between heats, or when the blast is shut off, the cinders are dropped from the tuyère iron into a cinder pit by opening the valve *f*, which is hinged at *h* and operated by the rod *k*.

The nozzle *v*, Fig. 1, and *b*, Fig. 2, with the valve *c* at the top of the tuyère iron, is called the **tuyère.** The valve is controlled by the handle shown at *k*, Fig. 1. A separate valve not shown in Fig. 2, but shown at *f*, Fig. 5, controls the amount of the opening for the air supply. The top of

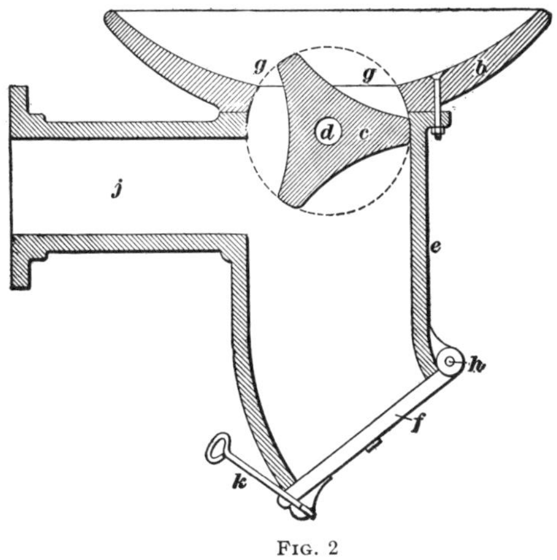

Fig. 2

the tuyère is usually so placed that it comes 3 or 4 inches below the level of the top of the brickwork, *a b c d*, Fig. 1, and from 12 to 15 inches in front of the chimney. The bottom of the fire space is occasionally covered with clay hollowed into a cup shape around the tuyère. In doing this, care must be taken to work, or temper, the clay to a proper consistency, for the stiffer it is, the less it will shrink and crack. Strong brine is often used to moisten the clay, as it keeps the bed from burning out too quickly. The space about the tuyère is also sometimes packed with cinders to the level of the tuyère. Suitable space is provided in the forge bottom for the free movement of the handles *k* and *s*, sometimes by incasing them in pieces of wrought-iron pipe.

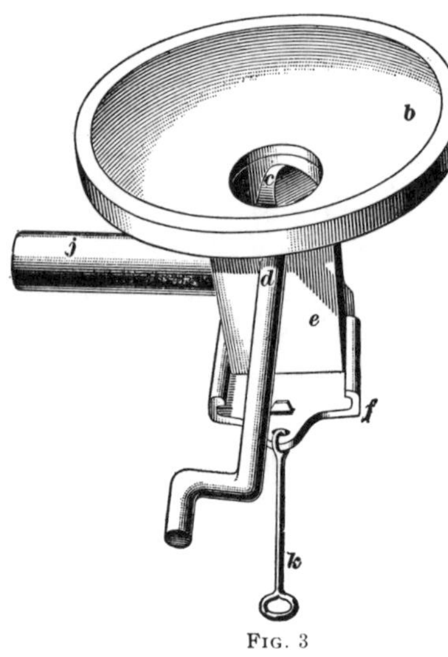

Fig. 3

Fig. 3 shows another common style of tuyère iron which is of cheaper and simpler construction than that shown in Fig. 2. The dish-shaped nozzle *b* has a circular hole in the bottom, below which is the valve *c*. By turning the rod *d*, the valve *c* is brought into different positions, thus increasing or diminishing the opening. The blast enters through the pipe *j*. The tube *e* is closed at the lower end by the shutter *f*. When cinders have collected in *e*, the shutter *f* is opened by means of the rod *k* and the cinders dropped out.

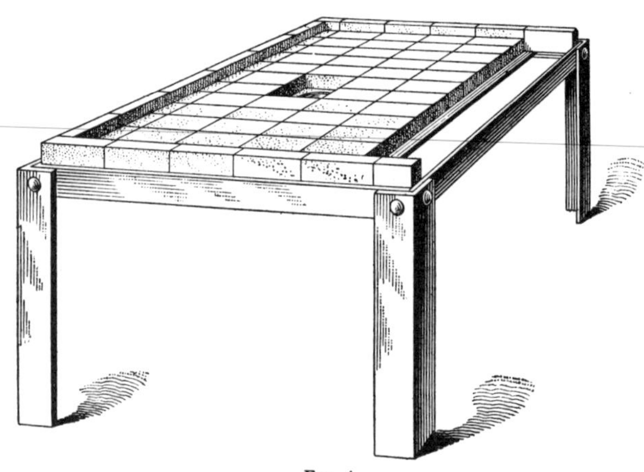
Fig. 4

3. Combination Forge.—Sometimes a combination brick and iron forge is made by supporting a frame of 2-inch or 3-inch angle iron, about $3\frac{1}{2}$ or 4 feet by 6 feet, on angle-iron legs, as shown in Fig. 4. The bottom is formed of $\frac{1}{2}'' \times 2''$ iron strips, supporting a layer of common red brick. The tuyère iron is attached to two of the $\frac{1}{2}$-inch iron strips, and the bottom of the hearth is covered with clay or cinders.

4. Iron Forge.—The iron forge is made with a cast-iron bowl supported on legs. The tuyère iron is fastened in the bottom of the bowl and the air blast is supplied either from a stationary blower, or bellows, or from a small blower secured to the forge. The blower may be driven by a crank, a treadle, or a lever working with a ratchet. Fig. 5 shows an iron forge which is suitable for either stationary or

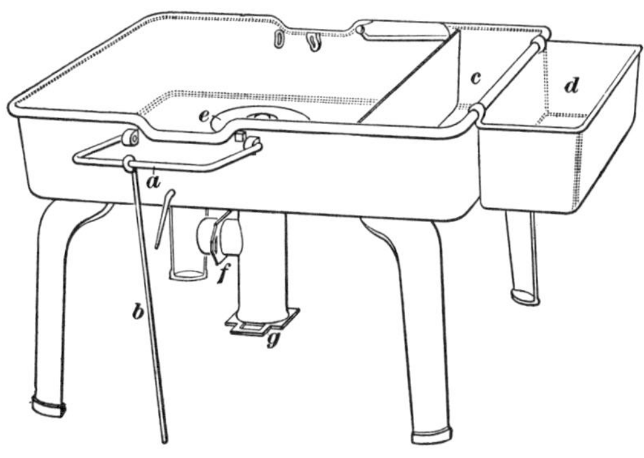

Fig. 5

portable use. It has no hood to obstruct the handling of the work. The blast is supplied from a blast pipe or from a small portable blower mounted on a separate stand; *a* is a rest for the tongs or long pieces of work; it is supported by the rod *b*; *c* is the coal trough and *d* the water trough; *e* is the top of the tuyère; *f* is the valve in the blast pipe; and *g* the cinder valve at the bottom of the tuyère iron.

PRODUCTION OF BLAST

5. The Bellows.—The air blast is produced either by means of a rotary fan or blower, or by a **bellows.** The bellows illustrated in Fig. 6 consists of two parts. These are separated by a partition, and the air from the lower half is forced through the valves *f* in the center board into the upper chamber, where it is stored for use. The bellows is hung from the center board by pins *m*, and as the lower board is drawn up, the air in the lower part is forced through the valves *f* into the upper chamber, inflating it and raising the top board. As the bottom board descends, the valves *f* close and the valves *c* open, allowing air to flow in and fill the space below the center board. By placing a weight on the top board, the air pressure in the upper part is increased. The top board should be held up when the bellows is idle for any great length of time, to keep the leather stretched to prevent it from cracking. This may be done

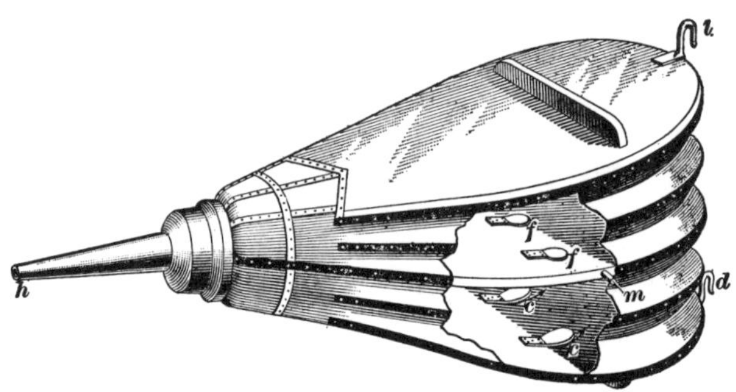

FIG. 6

by fastening the hook *l* in a chain suspended from the ceiling. With this care, the bellows will last much longer, for if the upper part is always folded together when not in use, the leather will soon crack and the upper part will be spoiled while the lower half is still in good condition. The operating chain or rod is attached to the hook *d*, and the air from the upper part discharges through the tube or nozzle *h*. The leather of the bellows should be oiled two or three times a year with neat's-foot oil or harness oil to preserve it. It should always be oiled before cold weather sets in, so as to make it pliable during the winter. On a cold morning, the bellows should be started slowly, so as not to crack the leather while it is stiff with the cold.

6. Rotary Blower or Fan.—The rotary blower or centrifugal fan, Fig. 7, has a number of blades set nearly radially on the shaft and placed within a cylindrical iron casing, with inlet holes *d* concentric with the shaft on each side, and an outlet, opening into the delivery pipe *k*, at the periphery of the casing. The shaft is driven by a belt passing over a pulley *e*. The centrifugal force, caused by the rapid rotation of the blades, throws the air outwards, that is, away from the center. The air close to the shaft rushes in through the opening *d*, to fill the space, and so a constant blast is maintained.

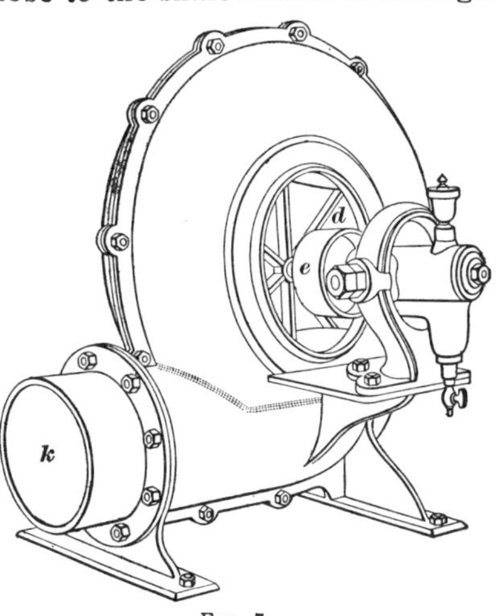

Fig. 7

For small forges, hand-driven rotary fans are very frequently used. There are a number of styles on the market driven by cranks either through trains of gears or through belts. These portable hand blowers, however, are used more in small smith shops than in black-smith shops connected with manufacturing plants. One of their principal advantages is that they take up less room than the bellows and are in many cases capable of producing a much greater blast pressure. A good hand blower should be so constructed that it can run in either direction without drawing ashes back into it. Power-driven fans may be operated by a belt from a pulley on the line shafting, by belting from an electric motor, or by direct-connected motor.

Several forms of **blast gates** are used in the blast pipes of power fans. These should be so placed that they may be conveniently operated by the smith while working at the forge. The blast gate, when closed, completely shuts off the air supply, but when opened, admits the blast to the tuyère; it can be set so as to supply the blast to suit the work. There are two general styles of gates for controlling the air pressure; one is an ordinary damper like that placed in a stovepipe, and the other is a slide that can be pushed in or drawn out through an opening in the side of the air pipe.

7. Positive Rotary Blower.—A positive blower differs from a fan in that it has two rotating pistons placed with their axes parallel and geared together at either one or both ends with gears of equal diameter. The pistons, or air impellers, have curved sides, and are so placed with reference to each other that they mesh correctly; they are, in fact, cycloidal gears with two teeth each. Because of this combination of form and arrangement of the pistons, the blast produced by the positive type of blower differs from that of the fan previously described. This blower delivers a definite quantity of air under pressure into the delivery pipe at each revolution of the pistons. Thus the air may be forced through an opening against resistance, such as a varying amount of cinders, coal, or metal covering a tuyère. A blast of this character is called a **positive blast,** and machines for producing it are called **positive blowers.**

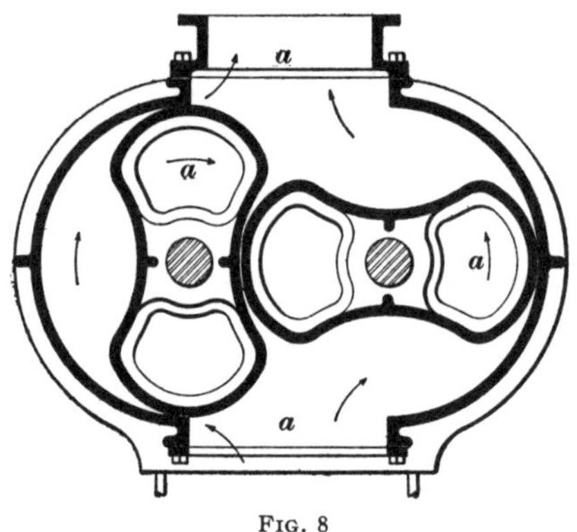

Fig. 8

Fig. 8 is a sectional view of one form of these rotary blowers taken at right angles to the axes of the pistons. The arrows at *a*, *a* show the directions of rotation of the pistons, and the direction of the air at the intake and delivery pipes. This same form of blower is sometimes connected to small forges and operated by hand.

8. Water Gauge.—For measuring the blast pressure, a **water gauge** is generally used. A simple form can be made by bending a $\frac{3}{8}$-inch glass tube to the shape shown in

Fig. 9. The tube is fastened to a board, and a scale, graduated in inches, is made to slide vertically between the two parallel arms of the tube. The air pipe, having a stop-cock at *s*, is then connected at *c* and the end *a* is left open. Water is poured into the tube until it rises to the height *d* in both tubes. The stop-cock *s* is then opened, and the air-blast pressure forces the water up in tube *a*; the scale is then moved into position so that the zero mark is on a line with the water level in the shorter tube, and the reading is taken at the level of the water in the long arm. Ordinarily, a blast of from 4 to 6 ounces pressure to the square inch, or, approximately, 7 to 10 inches of water, is used for a blacksmith's forge. A pressure of 1 pound to the square inch is equal to the pressure of a column of water with an area of 1 square inch and 27.7 inches high; and the pressure of 1 ounce to the square inch is equal to a pressure of 1.73 inches of water.

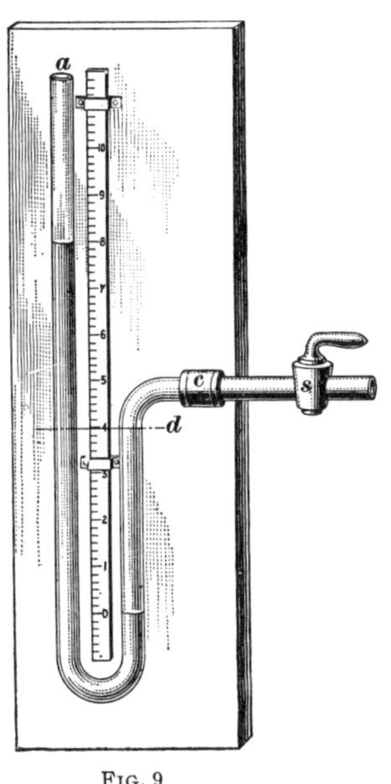

FIG. 9

DISPOSAL OF SMOKE AND GASES

9. Hoods and Chimneys.—In the case of a single stationary forge like that shown in Fig. 1, the gas and smoke from the fire are usually drawn up through the hood by the natural draft of the chimney. Where the forge stands in the center of the room, the hood is sometimes suspended over it and connected with a sheet-iron chimney going straight up through the roof. If these chimneys are provided with some form of top which will insure a draft no matter which way the wind blows, they are quite efficient.

10. Overhead Exhaust System.—In the overhead exhaust system, a hood is hung over each fire and the pipes from the hoods are carried to a common exhaust pipe, from which the smoke is drawn by means of a fan. This system is positive in its action and gives quite efficient service, but the suspended hoods and pipes are frequently in the way of cranes or other handling devices; they also obstruct the light to a certain degree.

11. Down-Draft System.—In the down-draft system, the hood is placed at one side of, and extending partly over, the fire, and is connected by an underground pipe with a fan, which draws the smoke and gases into the hood and through the pipe. A forge arranged for use with this system is shown in Fig. 10. Sometimes the fan that exhausts the smoke is so arranged that it returns a portion of the smoke and air to the forge as an air blast. As ten or twelve times as much air as smoke enters the hood, the mixture does very well for air blast. Besides, it has the advantage of being warm. When this system is used only one fan is necessary, the portion of the air and smoke not needed for the forge blast being delivered outdoors. Sometimes, however, it is preferred to use independent fans for the exhaust and the blast; and as the blast is always required at a higher pressure than is necessary at the outlet of the exhaust fan, it is probable that the double-fan system is the better for large shops. The greatest advantage of the down-draft system is that the space above the forge is clear for the use of cranes or handling devices, and that there are no pipes to obstruct the light.

Fig. 10

12. Blast Pipes.—The fan or blower should be located as close to the forge as possible, and care should be taken to avoid unnecessary bends in the pipe, because there will be considerable loss in pressure when forcing air through a long pipe or one having abrupt bends. The bends, if any, should be made in easy curves. In cases where a large number of forges are supplied with air from one fan, or blower, care must be taken to proportion the various branches of the pipe system correctly. The fan or blower must be run at a speed that will give more than 4 ounces pressure near the fan, in order to allow for the loss of pressure in the pipe and insure the proper pressure at the tuyère. The manufacturers of fans and blowers furnish tables giving the proper sizes and proportions of blast pipes.

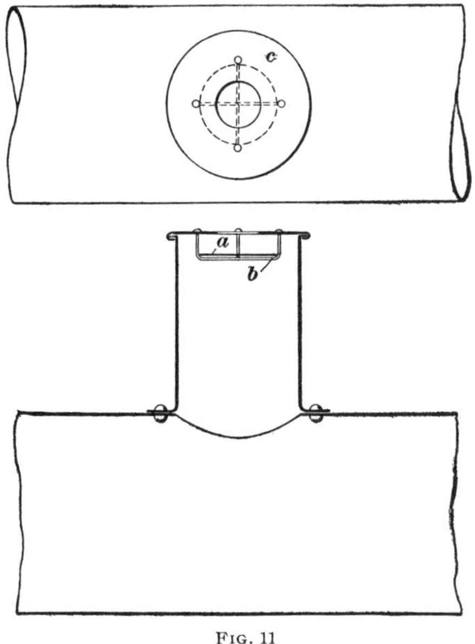

FIG. 11

13. Danger of Explosion.—Sometimes coal gas works back into the blast pipe when the fan is not running, as at noon, forming a mixture of gas and air that may explode and burst the pipe when the fan is started. This is particularly the case if the blast pipe is overhead. The danger of explosion may be prevented by having one or more valves in the top of the pipe, as shown in Fig. 11, to allow the gas to escape. The valve *a* is made of thin sheet iron, and is held up by the blast when the fan is running, but drops on cross-wires *b* and permits the gas to escape when the fan is not running. A top view of this valve is shown at *c*; it is 3 inches or more in diameter.

14. Ventilation.—The ventilation of large blacksmith shops in which heavy work is done is a difficult problem. Probably the best way of warming is by hot air blown into the shop through numerous openings near the floor. This tends to provide fresh air near the floor, while the smoke may be removed from the upper part of the room either by opening ventilators, or overhead windows, or by the use of fans. Sometimes all these methods are used together.

PORTABLE FORGES

15. Portable forges are those that may be moved about easily. They are of various designs and constructions, in order to meet the requirements of special classes of work. For example, some classes of work might have to be done by blacksmiths, others by machinists, bridge builders, boilermakers, etc. There are many kinds of work to which these forges are adapted, but they are especially useful when work is done away from the shop.

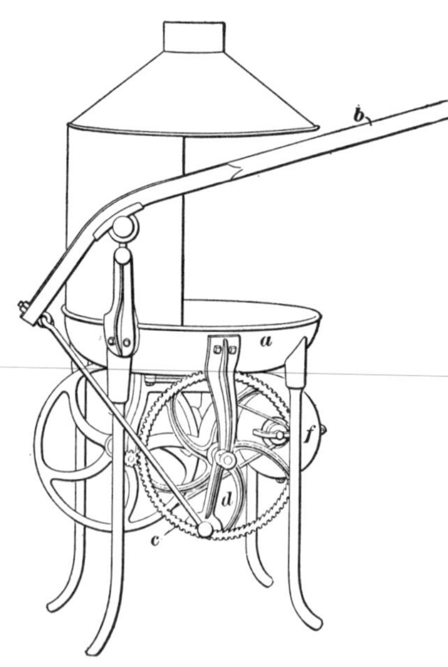

Fig. 12

Fig. 12 shows a portable forge that is much used for heating rivets. It has a cast-iron bowl *a* supported on legs made of iron pipe. The blast is supplied from a small rotary fan *f*, secured beneath the bowl. The fan is operated by the lever *b*, connected with a second lever *d*, which carries a ratchet on its outer end that engages with ratchet teeth on the inside of the gear *c*.

FORGE FIRES

FUELS

16. Coal.—The **fuel** that is most commonly used on blacksmiths' forges is **bituminous coal,** usually called **soft coal.** It is broken into small pieces, and when free from sulphur and phosphorus and of good quality is excellent for this purpose. A fuel containing either sulphur or phosphorus should be avoided, as they will be absorbed by the iron. Sulphur makes the iron **hot short,** that is, it makes it brittle while hot; and phosphorus makes it **cold short,** that is, brittle when cold.

Some grades of bituminous coal burn too rapidly, and some contain too much earthy matter to give a free-burning, clean fire producing a proper heat.

Anthracite culm or hard-coal siftings may be used at times, but this fuel is apt to contain a larger percentage of impurities than soft coal. In order to use it, careful attention must be given to the blast, and in any case it will not make a hollow fire.

17. Coke.—Coke is a solid fuel made from bituminous coal by heating it in the fire or in ovens until its volatile or gaseous constituents are driven off, the solid portion not being consumed. If the coal contains sulphur and phosphorus, these impurities will always exist in the coke, although a portion of the sulphur may have been driven off by the heat in coking.

18. Charcoal.—Another solid fuel made by artificial means is **charcoal.** It is the best fuel because of the small amount of impurities that it contains. It is unrivaled for heating carbon steels, giving a clean fire, free from sulphur and other objectionable matter. A charcoal fire is, however, not suitable for heating high-speed steels, as it is impossible to get the high temperature required. Charcoal made of maple or other hardwood is the best. Some manufacturers of twist drills, reamers, milling and other cutting tools, use charcoal exclusively. The objections to this fuel are that its cost is high and that it heats the work more slowly than coal.

FIRE AND FIRE-TOOLS

19. The Fire.—In the combustion of fuel (charcoal, coal, or coke), the oxygen of the air combines chemically with the carbon of the fuel. This chemical combination produces heat; the temperature attained depends on the rapidity with which the combination takes place, and the amount of heat depends on the amount of carbon and oxygen combined within a given period of time. Under ordinary conditions, the combustion would not go on rapidly enough to generate sufficient heat to raise iron or steel to the temperature necessary for working it under the hammer. Hence, the draft must be increased in order to supply more oxygen to the fuel, and thus increase the rate of combustion. It is possible, however, to supply too much air and blow out the fire, because too much cold air will chill the hot coals below the temperature at which the oxygen will combine with the carbon; or it may only lower the temperature by using the heat of the fire to warm the excess of air that passes through it. The greatest objection, however, to an excess of air is that too much oxygen will be supplied to the fire, and some of it will combine with the hot iron, forming **oxide of iron,** which is the black scale that falls from heated iron while being forged. A fire supplied with an excess of air is called an **oxidizing fire,** but if all the oxygen is used in the combustion and there is an excess of carbon, the fire is called a **reducing fire.**

A good way to start the fire is to heap coal all around the tuyère to a depth of 2 or 3 inches, leaving the tuyère uncovered. A handful of shavings or some oily waste is set on fire and put into the opening over the tuyère, and a small quantity of fuel is spread over it. The blast is turned on very lightly, and as the fire burns up, more fuel is added, and the blast is increased. A conical block of wood is sometimes used. The block is put over the tuyère with the small end down, and the coal packed about it. The block is then taken out and shavings put into its place, and the fire started.

If coal is used for fuel, it is well to coke a quantity of it before putting the iron into the fire. The fire is kept from spreading by sprinkling water around the edges. The fire should not be allowed to burn too low, because this makes it necessary to place the iron nearer the tuyère and brings the hot iron too near the cold blast. For this reason, the blast must always have a good bed of fire to pass through before coming in contact with the iron that is being heated. The hot iron should not come in contact with the fresh coal. As the fuel is burned, the coke is brought toward the center and

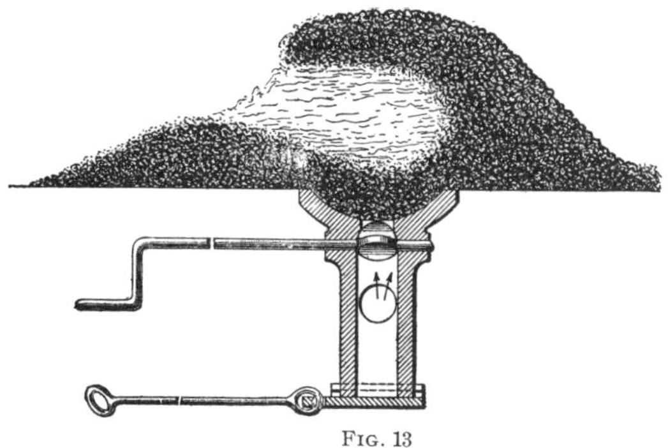

Fig. 13

fresh fuel is added on the outside of the heap, where it can coke slowly. The fire must always be kept clean, all cinders, ashes, and scraps of iron being removed. Care should be taken to prevent lead and Babbitt metal from getting into the fire, as they are objectionable, particularly if welding is to be done.

If the fire is not to be used for some time, it may be held by putting a stick of hardwood into the fire and pounding the fuel down around it. The blast is then turned on gently for a few moments to liven it up well. After this, it may be left without a blast for an hour or more, and can be restarted by turning on the blast. The ashes and cinders are then raked out and blown out with the blast, or dropped through the tuyère into the cinder pit.

20. Forms of Fire.—The fire may be maintained either open or hollow. In the **open fire,** the combustion takes place on top of the heap over the tuyère; while in the **hollow fire,** a section of which is shown in Fig. 13, the combustion takes place inside, the top being roofed over with coke and coal. A hole is left in front for the iron. The advantages of the hollow fire are that it is much hotter than the open fire, as the hot roof radiates heat as well as the hot sides and bottom, and it also heats the iron more evenly, and thus lessens the chilling by contact with the outside air.

21. Fire-Tools.—The following fire-tools should be provided for each forge: A **poker,** Fig. 14 (*a*), which is a

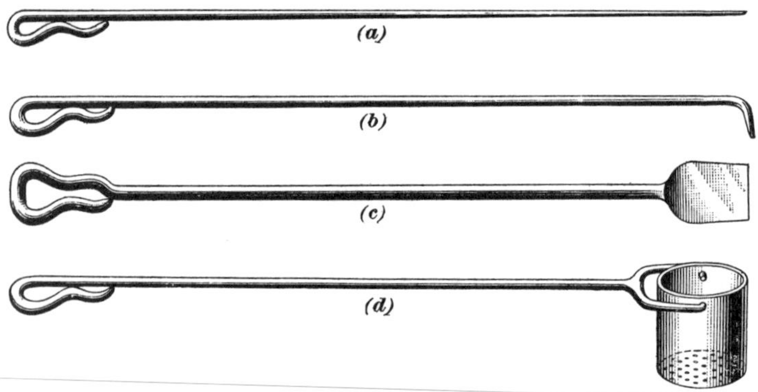

FIG. 14

rod of iron or steel about $\frac{1}{2}$ inch in diameter and at least 20 inches long, with a handle at one end; a **fire-hook,** Fig. 14 (*b*), which is similar to the poker, but has a hook bent on one end; a **shovel,** Fig. 14 (*c*), which has a sheet-iron blade and a long handle; and a **sprinkler,** Fig. 14 (*d*), which consists of a forked iron handle sprung into holes in a tin can, the bottom of the can having holes punched in it for the escape of the water. This is used for cooling parts or pieces of iron and for keeping the fire from spreading.

BLACKSMITHING TOOLS

THE ANVIL

22. Construction of the Anvil.—The ordinary blacksmith's **anvil** is shown in Fig. 15. It has a horn *a* on one end, around which bending is done. The body of the anvil may be made either of wrought iron, or of a special quality of cast iron, or it may be a steel casting. The top is faced with steel, which is sometimes planed true and then hardened, or first brought approximately to shape and then hardened and finished by grinding. Anvils having cast-iron bodies usually have unhardened steel horns, which are tough and not easily broken. Anvils having wrought-iron bodies usually have horns of the same material. It is claimed that the cast-iron body gives a firmer backing for the steel face of the anvil than does wrought iron. The face of steel is usually hardened under a flow of water. If too soft, it will nick; and if too hard, it is liable to chip at the corners and edges. Anvils made of the usual qualities of cast iron are brittle. A cast-iron anvil with a horn of the same material cannot be used for heavy work because the horn is liable to be broken off, which is not the case with the wrought-iron anvil. For light work, however, the cast-iron anvil will give good service.

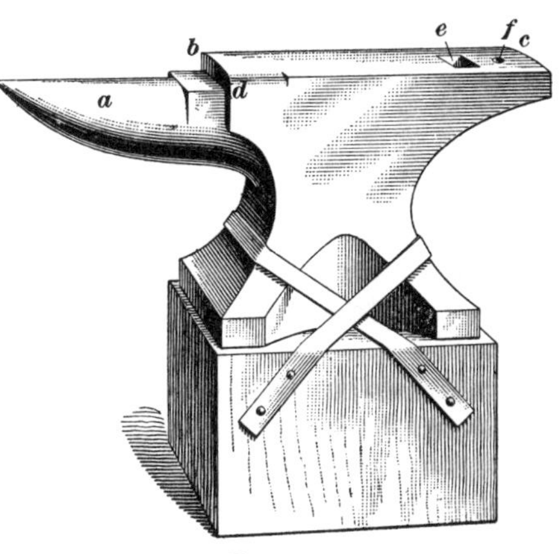

FIG. 15

Square-faced anvils without horns are frequently made of cast iron, but the edges chip off easily.

The face of the anvil is straight lengthwise, as shown from *b* to *c*, Fig. 15, but it is slightly crowned crosswise from *b* to *d*, as shown somewhat exaggerated. If the face of the anvil were perfectly flat, a straight piece of iron would show a tendency to curl upwards while being hammered when held crosswise of the anvil, and unless it were held perfectly flat on the anvil it would sting the hand; besides, there would be danger of nicking the iron where it rests on the corner of the anvil. When hammering a piece of iron on the crowned face of an anvil, the effect of the blow is more nearly confined to that part of the face where the hammer strikes; thus the crowned face acts to some extent like a bottom fuller, which is described later. A portion of the edge of the face is sometimes rounded, as shown at *d*.

At the right-hand end of the anvil there is a square hole *e* called the **hardie hole,** in which cutting and forming tools are held. The small round hole *f* near it is called the **pritchel hole;** the core of small holes is punched out through it.

23. Setting an Anvil.—The anvil should be placed on a solid block of wood, preferably a butt end of oak, and should be fastened to it with iron straps, as shown in Fig. 15, or with staples. Anvils on which soft metals are to be worked often have a layer of leather, felt, or cloth beneath them. The height of an anvil should be such that when the workman stands beside it his knuckles will just reach its face.

24. The Weight of Anvils.—The weights of anvils vary greatly; small ones are used for light work and large ones for heavy work. An average anvil will weigh from 150 to 200 pounds. Formerly, most of the anvils used in the United States were imported from England. These generally have the weight stamped on the side, and on many anvils it is given in hundredweights of 112 pounds each. If a person stands facing the anvil, with the horn to the right, the weight is generally found stamped on the near side; the figures toward the left designate the number of hundredweights of

112 pounds; the figures in the center denote the quarters of a hundredweight; and the figures at the right side show the number of extra pounds. Thus, if an anvil is stamped 2–2–17, it means 2 hundredweight of 112 pounds each, which is 224 pounds, 2 quarters of a hundredweight, which is 56 pounds, and 17 pounds, making the total weight of the anvils 224 + 56 + 17 = 297 pounds. However, the present practice among American makers is to stamp their anvils with the direct weight in pounds.

HAND TOOLS

HAMMERS AND SLEDGES

25. Classification.—Hammers are classified, according to weight, as *hand hammers*, *hand sledges*, and *swing sledges;* according to the peen, into *ball-peen*, shown in Fig. 16 (*a*), *cross-peen*, shown in Fig. 16 (*b*), and *long-peen*, or *straight-peen*, shown in Fig. 16 (*c*).

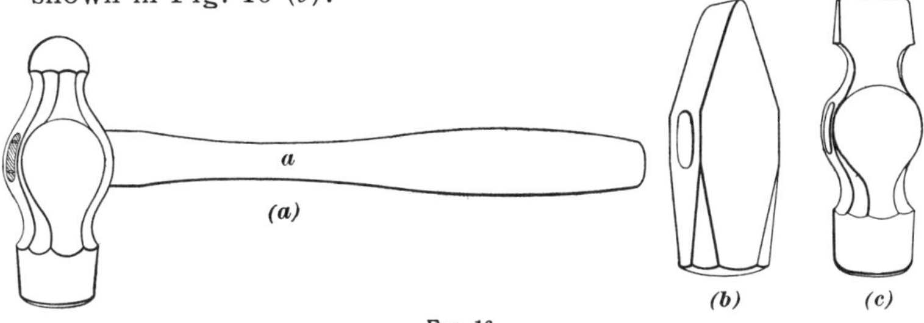

FIG. 16

26. Hand Hammers.—The hand hammer is made to use with one hand and is handled by the smith himself. It should not weigh more than 2½ pounds, a 1-pound hammer being a very convenient size for small work. The handle should be well formed, elliptical or oval in section, and a little thinner toward the head, as shown at *a*, Fig. 16 (*a*); this is done to give it a spring, in order to avoid stinging the hand. It is from 14 to 16 inches long, and is made of a size that will fit the hand comfortably. A handle of improper shape is apt to tire or cramp the hand. It should be durable, not a makeshift, for the smith soon becomes accustomed to a hammer, and knows what effect a blow will have. It is dangerous to use a hammer with a loose head.

27. Hand Sledge.—A hand sledge, shown in Fig. 17, is larger than the hand hammer. It weighs from 5 to 8 pounds and is used by the helper, who holds it with both hands. The handle is from 26 to 34 inches long, and not so slender, in proportion, as the handle of the hand hammer. In striking with the hand sledge, the helper holds it in both hands and strikes a shoulder blow; that is, he raises the head of the sledge to the shoulder and strikes from this position. Both large hammers and hand sledges are frequently called *flogging* hammers.

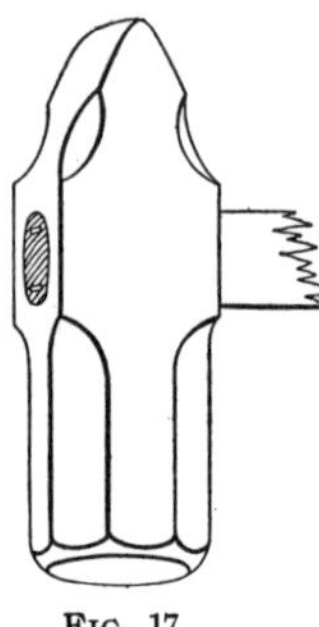

Fig. 17

28. Swing Sledge.—The swing sledge, one form of which is shown in Fig. 18, weighs from 8 to 20 pounds, or more. The handle is about 3 feet long. In using the swing sledge, the helper grasps the handle near the end with both hands, and strikes a full-arm-swing blow. This sledge is used for striking a heavy blow. The swing sledge is also made of the form shown in Fig. 17.

29. Ball-Peen Hammer.—The ball-peen, or **chipping hammer,** shown in Fig. 16 (*a*), is a hand hammer that has the peen in the shape of a ball. The peen is used in riveting, or where it is required to stretch the metal in length and width, or for working in a hollow.

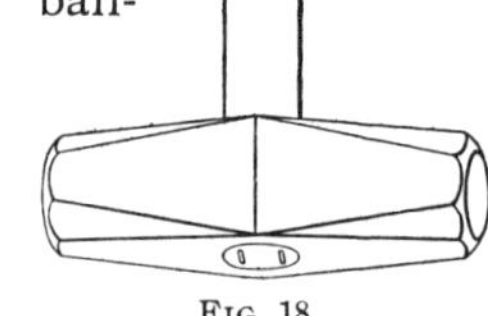

Fig. 18

30. Cross-Peen Hammer.—The cross-peen hammer, shown in Fig. 16 (*b*), is used when it is required to stretch the metal lengthwise, but not crosswise. The cross-peen hand hammer is also used for riveting.

31. Long- or Straight-Peen Hammer.—The long-peen or straight-peen hammer, shown in Fig. 16 (*c*), is used when the metal is to be spread sidewise. These hammers are made of different weights, and are selected to suit the work and the strength of the smith; a good set of hand hammers consists of a 1-pound ball-peen, a 1½-pound straight-peen, and a 2-pound cross-peen hammer.

32. Material Used for Hammers.—Hammers were formerly made of wrought iron or mild steel and faced with tool steel. If the whole head is made of tool steel, it is liable to chip and crack, but with a soft backing this is avoided to a great extent. Hammers made of a special cast steel, called hammer steel, are much used at present, and give entire satisfaction.

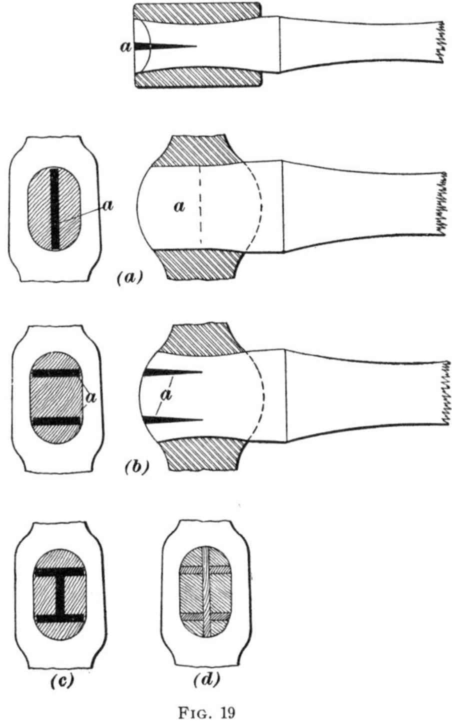

Fig. 19

33. Hammer Handles.—Hammer handles should be made of the best quality of white, straight-grained, second-growth hickory that has been well seasoned. The handle should be carefully fitted to the eye in the hammer head so that it fills the eye as nearly as possible. The handle must also be at right angles to the hammer head, so that when striking a blow the head will fall squarely, and not on the edge.

The eye in the hammer head is generally made larger at its ends than at the middle. When the end of the handle is properly wedged, it will spread in the eye and hold the handle securely in the head. The eye is widened sidewise, or lengthwise, and often in both directions from the middle of the head toward the outside.

If the widening is sidewise only, but one wedge is used, as shown at *a*, Fig. 19 (*a*). If widened at the top and bottom, and not at the sides, two wedges are driven crosswise as shown at *a*, Fig. 19 (*b*). If the widening is in both directions, three iron wedges are used, as shown in Fig. 19 (*c*), or three wooden wedges, as shown in Fig. 19 (*d*).

FORMING AND CUTTING TOOLS

34. Set Hammers.—When a piece of work is of such shape that it cannot be reached so as to do the work properly with a hammer, a **set hammer** is used. The face of the

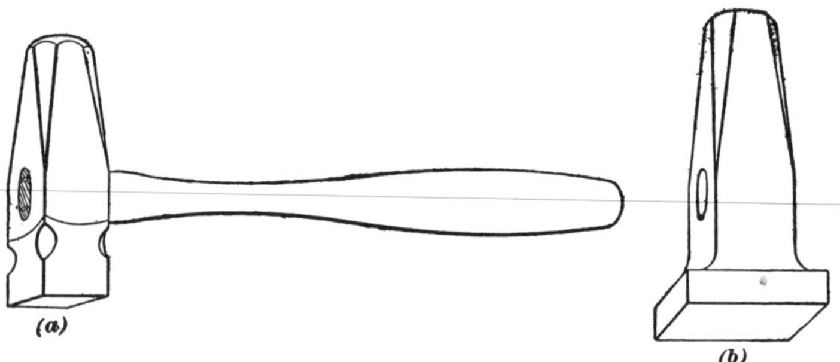

Fig. 20

set hammer is placed on the part of the work where the blow is desired, and the other end receives the hammer or sledge blow. Sometimes a set hammer is used to prevent marring the work, or to give some part of the work a definite form not readily obtained with the hammer. The faces of set hammers are formed into special shapes to suit the requirements of the various classes of work. The square set hammer shown in Fig. 20 (*a*) is used to produce a flat surface, or make a square shoulder or offset.

35. Flatter.—The flatter, shown in Fig. 20 (*b*), is used for the same class of work as the square set hammer, the distinction between the two being that the flatter has a larger face. For this reason, the flatter is used to flatten down a surface in finishing, while the square set hammer is preferable when a square shoulder is to be made and the iron well driven down.

36. Fuller.—The fuller, shown in Fig. 21 (*a*), is used in spreading the iron. Owing to its shape it concentrates

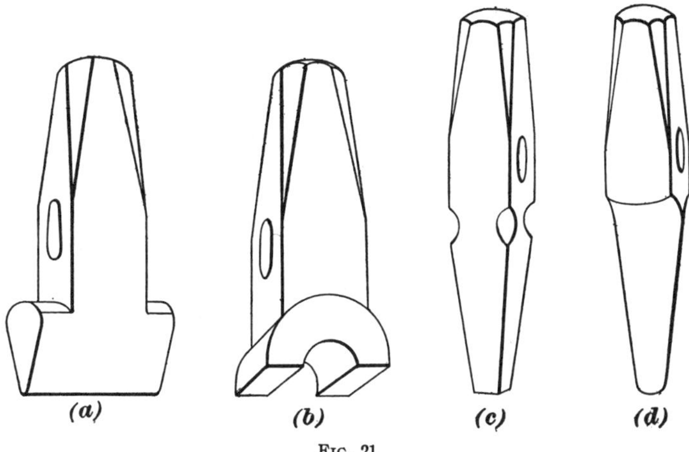

FIG. 21

the force of the sledge blow on a small surface and therefore makes it more effective at that place. The fuller spreads the iron at right angles to the working edges. Its action is the same as that of the cross-peen or long-peen hammer. It is also used for hollowing out work.

37. Swage.—One form of swage, also called a **collar tool,** is shown in Fig. 21 (*b*). Swages are often used in pairs, with the lower half, called the **bottom swage,** placed on the anvil with its square shank in the hardie hole.

The swage is usually a grooved tool, and is used principally for forming and shaping bar iron or rods into circular or hexagonal sections. It is also used for forming flanges or collars on rods. Each swage is made for a section of a certain size. An assortment of four or more swages is generally kept at hand, hexagonal swages being used on bolt heads having six sides.

38. Punches.—Fig. 21 (*c*) shows a square punch, and Fig. 21 (*d*) shows a round punch. The punch is tapered, being small at the point and increasing in size toward the handle. The hole is made by driving the punch into the iron, and is then stretched by driving the punch through the work until the desired size is obtained.

39. Cutters.—A cold cutter, to be used with a wooden handle, is shown in Fig. 22 (*a*), and a **hot cutter** in Fig. 22 (*b*). The cutting edge of the cold cutter is slightly convex, and is ground so that it is more blunt than the edge of the hot cutter. The hot cutter is drawn out thinner than the cold cutter, and its edge is sharper. It is used for cutting hot metal. When properly tempered and ground, the cold cutter should hold its edge when cutting cold iron or steel. When used for this purpose, it is frequently called a **flogging chisel.** The cold cutter cuts, or nicks, and at the same time wedges the edges of the cut apart, while the hot cutter makes the cut as narrow as possible so as not to batter the cut ends. The cold cutter is used to nick the metal all around so that it can be broken. The cutting edge should be lubricated frequently by pressing it into a piece of oiled waste or by dipping it into water.

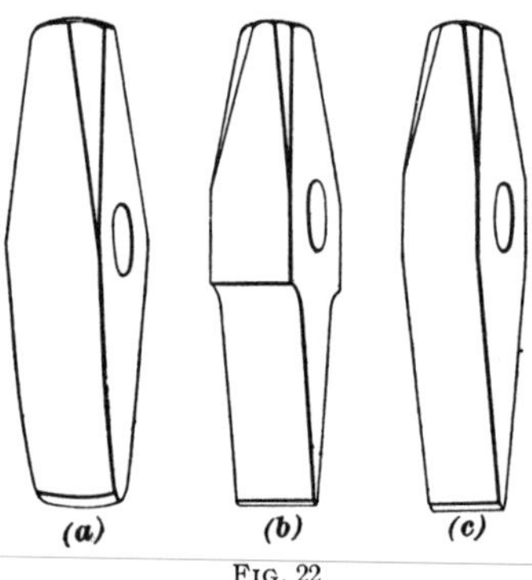

FIG. 22

40. For cutting off rivet heads, a cold cutter, similar to the punch shown in Fig. 21 (*d*), is used. The end of the tool is formed at a slight angle from the flat, varying from

20° to 30°, and the center of the face is slightly hollowed. For cutting down a straight surface, the side cutter shown in Fig. 22 (*c*) is frequently used. These side cutters are made either right or left.

ANVIL TOOLS

41. There are a number of tools, made to fit into the hardie hole, that correspond in shape to the set hammers.

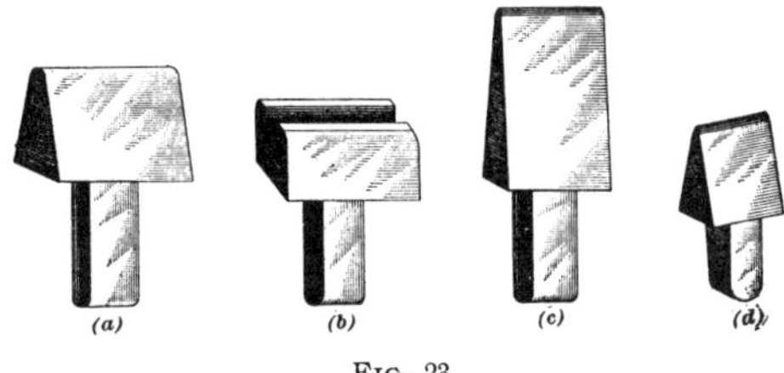

FIG. 23

The results obtained with them are similar to the results obtained with the corresponding set hammers. Fig. 23 (*a*) shows a **bottom fuller,** which, like the top fuller, is intended to spread or stretch the iron. The shank of the fuller fits into the hardie hole of the anvil.

Fig. 23 (*b*) shows a **bottom swage** with a single groove. It is similar to the top swage, and they are ordinarily used together. Bottom swages are frequently made with two or three grooves of different sizes in the same block.

The **hot hardie** is shown in Fig. 23 (*c*) and the **cold hardie** in Fig. 23 (*d*). They correspond in shape to the hot and cold cutters. The hot hardie, being slender and ground to a thin edge, is suitable for making a sharp, clean cut; the cold hardie is thicker and its edge is ground more blunt, so that it may have proper strength to cut cold iron or steel.

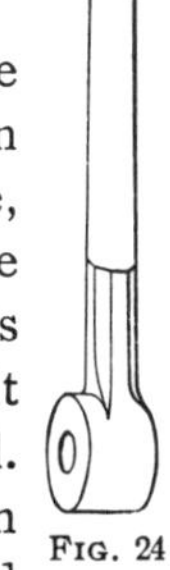

FIG. 24

The **heading tool,** shown in Fig. 24, is used in forming heads on the ends of rods, bars, bolts, and similar work. The hole through the head is usually circular or square. There should be an assortment of these heading tools on hand to fit the various sizes of iron bars. The hole should be from $\frac{1}{32}$ to $\frac{1}{16}$ inch larger than the iron; $\frac{1}{32}$ inch in the case of $\frac{1}{2}$-inch diameter, increasing to $\frac{1}{16}$ inch on $1\frac{1}{4}$-inch and larger diameters.

TONGS

42. Tongs are used for handling pieces of hot iron of various forms. A few of the most common kinds are mentioned below. Special tongs are made to fit special forms, and it is frequently necessary to make a new pair or to alter a pair to fit some oddly shaped piece of iron. The parts of the tongs, Fig. 25 (*a*), are the *jaws a* and the handles *b*, sometimes called the *reins*. An oval ring *a*, Fig. 25 (*d*), called the *coupler*, is frequently slipped over the handles to hold the work tight, and thus relieve the hand from the more severe part of the holding strain.

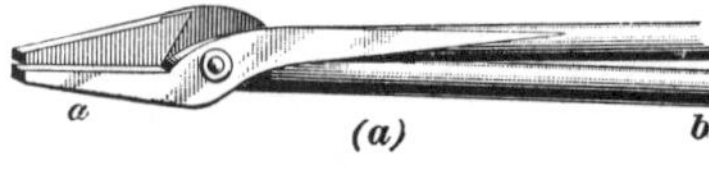

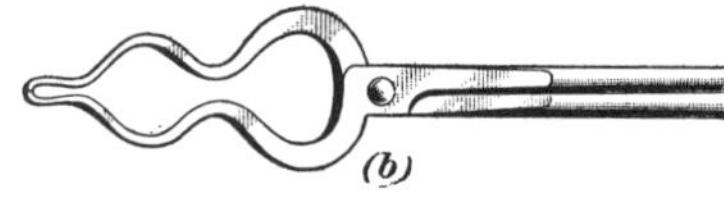

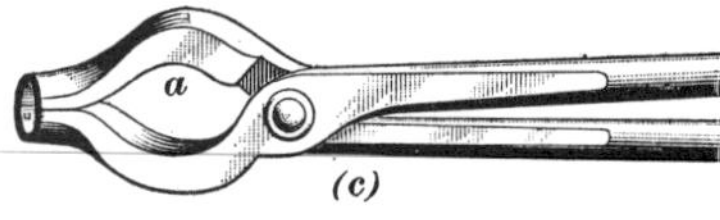

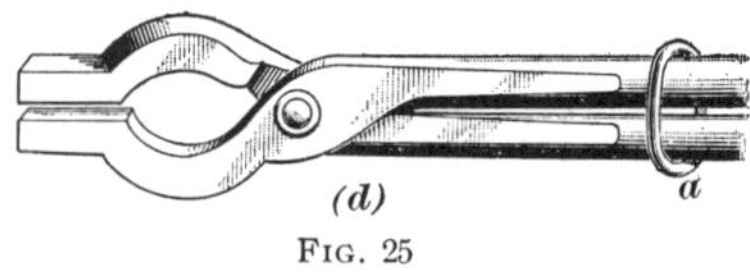

Fig. 25

The tongs should always be hung on a rack placed near at hand to prevent their being mislaid. The jaws should not be left in the fire if it can be avoided, for when they become hot they will bend apart and must be bent back before they can be used again, and besides they must be dipped into water. Repeated heating and dipping makes the iron brittle and spoils it.

Fig. 25 (*a*) shows a pair of **flat tongs** used for holding flat iron. When closed tightly, the jaws should always be parallel and have full-face bearing on the piece of iron being held.

Fig. 25 (*b*) shows a pair of **pick-up tongs** used for pick ing up pieces of iron, also for holding small pieces while tempering, etc. The jaws are bent to give them spring and the front bend is convenient for holding round iron.

Fig. 25 (*c*) shows a pair of **bolt tongs.** They are made for holding round iron and have a *pocket*, *a*, for the head of the bolt.

The **gad tongs,** shown in Fig. 25 (*d*), are used for holding flat or wedge-shaped pieces that have a head or large end.

Fig. 26 illustrates a form of tongs that has the lower jaw

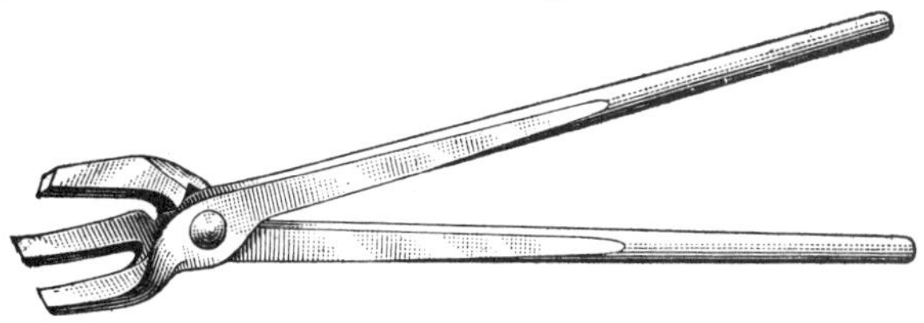

Fig. 26

divided into two prongs, while the upper jaw is **V**-shaped. The pressure of the upper jaw on the work being held comes between the prongs of the lower jaw. These tongs will hold round, octagon, square, and flat pieces of work with a firm grip when proper-sized tongs are used.

FLOOR AND BENCH TOOLS

43. Swage Blocks.—Figs. 27 and 28 show two forms of cast-iron **swage blocks.** These blocks have variously shaped grooves and holes cut into them, and are used like a swage or as a heading tool, and for similar work. They are really simple forms of dies. Fig. 28 shows a swage block on a stand. The grooves *h*, *h* in the edges are used for forming hexagonal heads and nuts of various sizes. The block may be turned on the stand to bring any side or edge up.

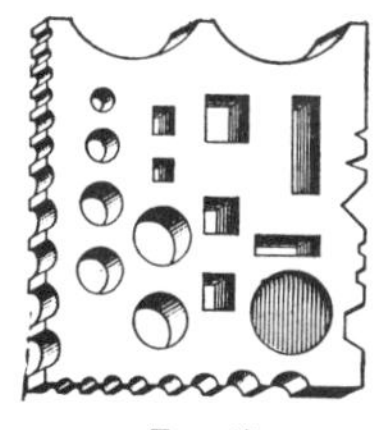

Fig. 27

44. Tapered Mandrel.—For forming rings and eyes, the **cone,** or **tapered mandrel,** shown in Fig. 29 (*a*) and (*b*), is largely used. It is made of cast iron and is formed of either one or two pieces. If it is formed of two pieces, as shown in Fig. 29 (*a*), the top piece, shown at the left and called the *tip*, is made with a shank on the bottom, which fits into the bottom piece and dowels the two parts together. The body *a* of the mandrel is given a plain smooth taper, but usually a groove *b* extends the entire length. This groove enables the smith to grasp the work with a pair of tongs while it is on the cone; or, in the case

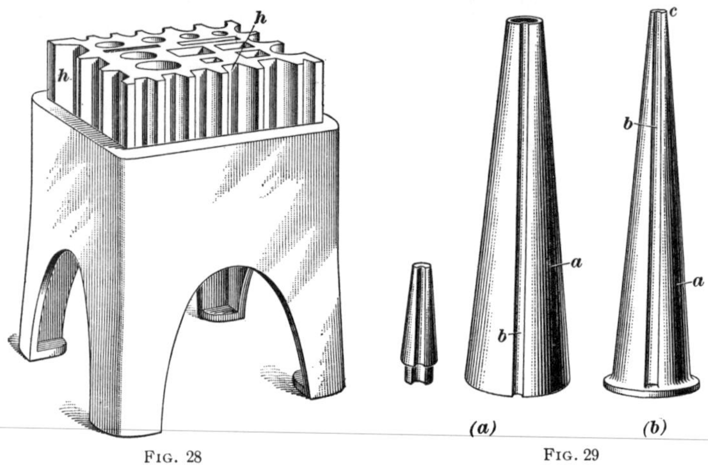

FIG. 28 FIG. 29

of a ring attached to a chain, or of an eye on a ring, the link or eye enters the groove. Some cones are so tapered that the upper end *c* is little more than 1 inch in diameter; the diameter of the lower end ordinarily varies between 8 and 14 inches. The height ranges between $2\frac{1}{2}$ and 5 feet. When the cone is made in two pieces, the shank of the tip may be placed in a vise to hold it firmly for bending small work.

45. Surface Plate.—The ordinary surface plate is made of cast iron, varying in thickness from $1\frac{1}{2}$ to 4 inches, and planed smooth on the top. This planed face is used for testing work—to see whether it is straight, and to detect warp or wind. It is also very useful in laying out work. The surface plate is generally placed on a small strong bench, as shown in Fig. 30, so as to be accessible from all sides. It should be carefully leveled and then secured in position; this makes it possible to test work on it by means of a level. Large surface plates are ribbed on the bottom to make them stiffer. Surface plates about 4 feet wide and 8 feet long are of convenient size for general use, the top being about $2\frac{1}{2}$ inches thick, with two side ribs around the bottom and several cross-ribs, making the total depth of the plate about 8 inches; these plates are used for rocker-shafts, yokes, and similar work. For use in shops where locomotive frames are made, plates about 4 or $4\frac{1}{2}$ feet wide by 20 or 24 feet long are used, made as shown in Fig. 31. The sides of these plates are 3 inches thick, and are connected by ribs as shown. The plate is planed on both sides, and may be turned over occasionally to keep it straight, as the hammering it gets tends to stretch the upper surface and make the plate high in the middle.

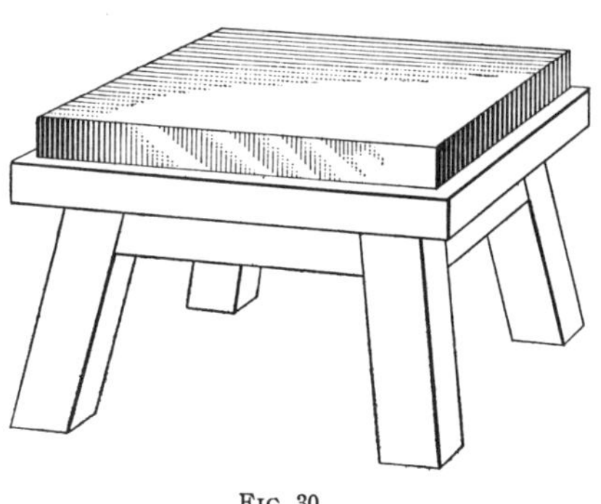

Fig. 30

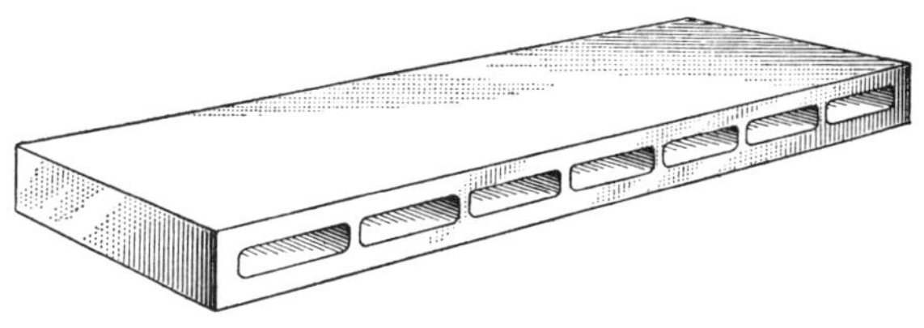

Fig. 31

46. Surface Gauge.—Fig. 32 shows a surface gauge that is used to scribe a line on a piece of work, *c*. This tool is used on the surface plate to draw, or scribe, lines parallel to the surface of the plate. The sliding collar *a* can be set at any height on the vertical standard *b*, and the needle *d* can be clamped in any position on this collar.

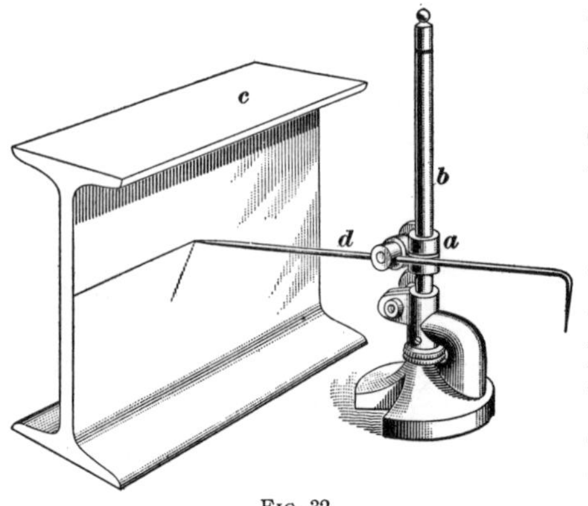

FIG. 32

47. Bench Vise. The vise is a tool in which the work is held securely for bending, twisting, chipping, filing, etc. The blacksmith's vise shown in Fig. 33 is called a **leg vise.** The leg rests in a solid block on the floor, while the body is secured to the bench with bolts through the strap *s*. The vise is made of wrought iron and has hardened-steel jaws. The screw has a square thread, and should be oiled occasionally. The top of the vise should be set at elbow height; this will be found most convenient for filing and chipping.

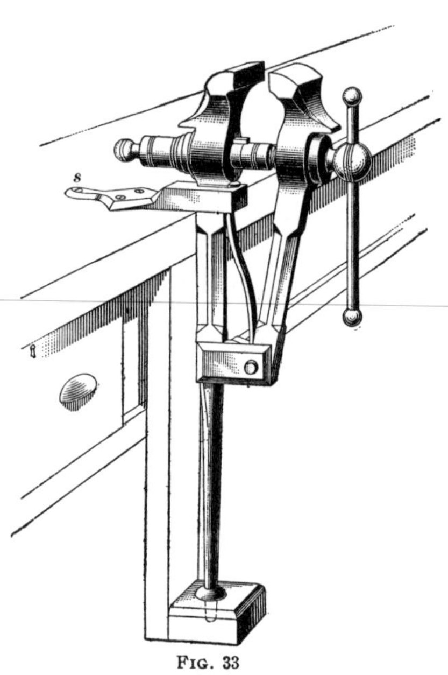

FIG. 33

48. Anvil Vise. In shops where heavy horseshoeing is done, a heavy 6-inch vise can, with advantage, be bolted to a 10″ × 10″ timber post set in the ground near the anvil. The jaws of the vise should be about the same height as the top of the anvil. A vise thus arranged has several uses, the principal one being to clamp the hot horseshoe while bending the heel calk.

49. Vise Jaws.—A very necessary addition to the vise is a pair of copper **vise jaws,** shown in Fig. 34. These are made of sheet copper, from $\frac{1}{16}$ to $\frac{1}{10}$ inch thick, formed to fit over and between the jaws of the vise. They protect the work from being bruised, as it would be if it were clamped between the bare jaws. Besides, they protect the jaws of the vise, for it is often necessary to clamp hot pieces of iron in the vise. This would draw the temper out of the jaws if they came in direct contact with it. To make them more efficient for this purpose, pieces of asbestos paper are placed over the jaws of the vise, under the copper jaws. This makes the insulation very good, and, besides protecting the steel jaws, prevents the rapid cooling of hot iron by contact with the cold vise. Sheet-iron jaws are often used for hot work.

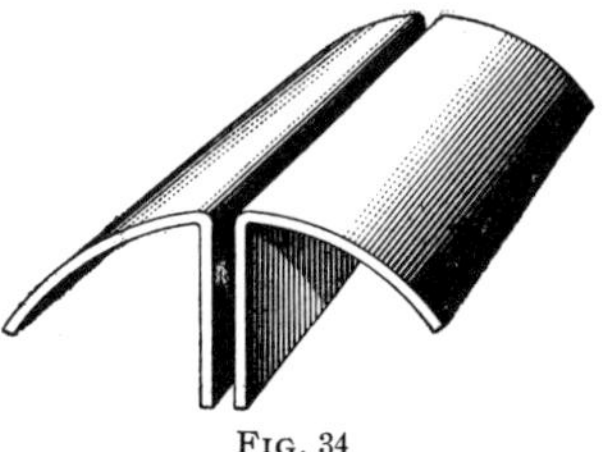

FIG. 34

50. Calipers. Calipers are used for measuring diameters, widths, and thicknesses. Single calipers are made of two pieces of sheet steel bent to the required shape and put together with a rivet. They are made to work rather stiffly, so as to remain wherever set. Fig. 35 (*a*) shows a pair of outside calipers, and Fig. 35 (*b*) a pair of inside calipers. Fig. 36 shows a pair of double calipers, which may be set

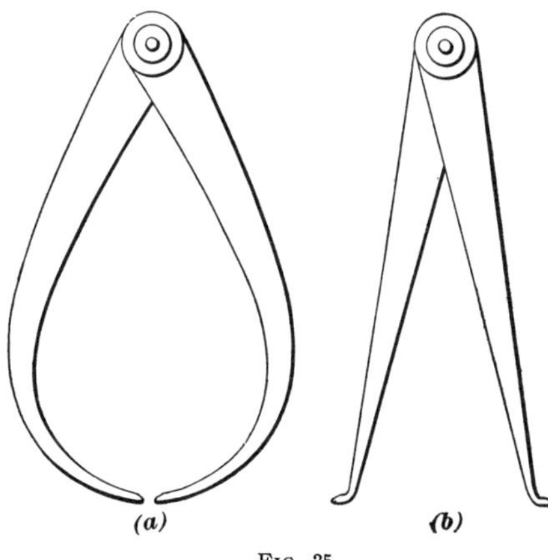

FIG. 35

for two sizes, as, for instance, the width and thickness of a forging.

51. Dividers.—The dividers, shown in Fig. 37, are

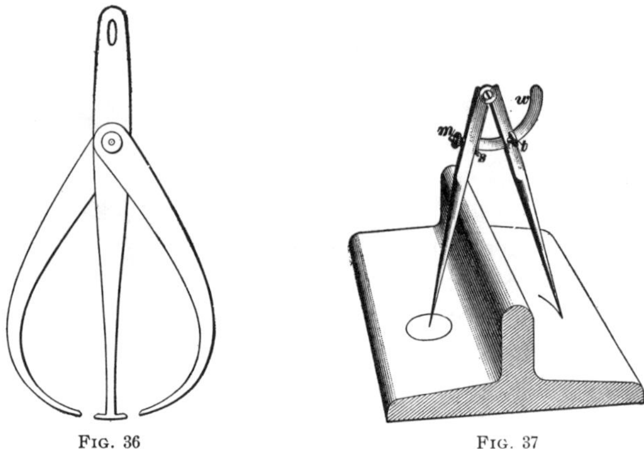

FIG. 36 FIG. 37

used for measuring the distance between two points and for describing circles. The points are clamped by means of a thumbscrew *t*, which bears against the wing *w*, and the finer adjustments are made by means of the thumb nut *m* The points are held apart by means of the spring *s*.

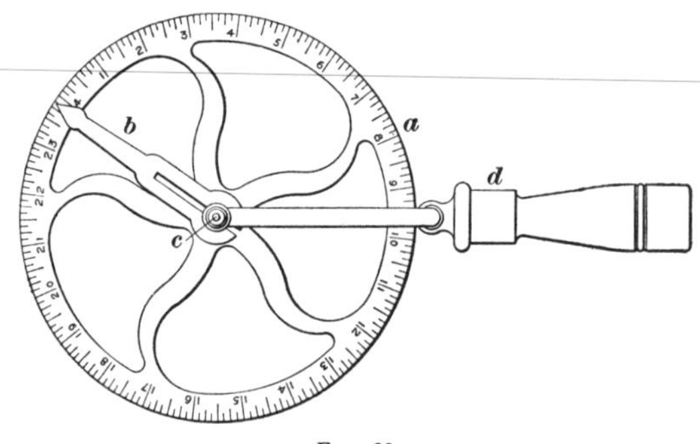

FIG. 38

52. Measuring Wheel, or Circular Rule.—The measuring wheel, or circular rule, shown in Fig. 38, also called a *traveler*, a *traverse wheel*, or a *tire wheel*, is usually a thin circular ring *a* about $\frac{1}{10}$ inch thick. Sometimes the hub consists of a thimble fitted into a hole in the center of the wheel. This thimble also forms the support for an index arm, or pointer *b*, which turns with the wheel and may be set to any point on its circumference. The spindle *c* on which the wheel turns is held between the ends of a forked handle *d*, as shown. Sometimes a boss is stamped on one side of the wheel to form the hub, which is threaded and fitted with a thumb nut to bear on the pointer and hold it in position. The measuring wheel is sometimes a drop forging turned true on the edge and having the division marks stamped on one side in the process of forging.

The wheel usually has a circumference of 24 inches, which is subdivided on one side into inches, halves, quarters, and eighths, the zero and 24-inch marks being at the same point. Sometimes, however, the wheel is plain with the exception of one short radial line on one side touching the circumference. The wheel is carefully rolled over the length of the work to be measured, the measurement being started at and read from the zero line. The pointer is moved to indicate the point on the circumference of the wheel where the measurement ends. The number of complete revolutions of the wheel must be counted. Chalk marks on a plain wheel often serve as substitutes for a zero line and pointer. On curved work, the wheel should be moved over the line of mean length, between the outside and inside measurements.

53. Marking Materials.—A soapstone pencil is the best material for making surface marks on iron, although chalk, slate pencils, and crayons are used for the purpose. Soapstone marks will not burn off, and the end of the pencil may be filed wedge-shaped and used to give a sharp clear line for laying out work. Soapstone pencils are made both round and rectangular in section; in either case, the pencil is usually from 5 to 6 inches long. The round pencils vary from $\frac{1}{4}$ to $\frac{3}{8}$ inch in diameter; the rectangular ones are usually $\frac{1}{4}$ inch thick by $\frac{1}{2}$ inch wide.

54. Scriber.—In some cases, it is desirable to scribe on the metal a line that will cut through the surface scale. To do this, a steel **scriber** of the general form shown in Fig. 39 is used. It is usually from $\frac{3}{16}$ to $\frac{1}{4}$ inch in diameter and from 6 to 8 inches long. The point must be quite hard, and the temper of the rest of the tool must be carefully drawn to secure the necessary elasticity and to prevent the point from breaking off.

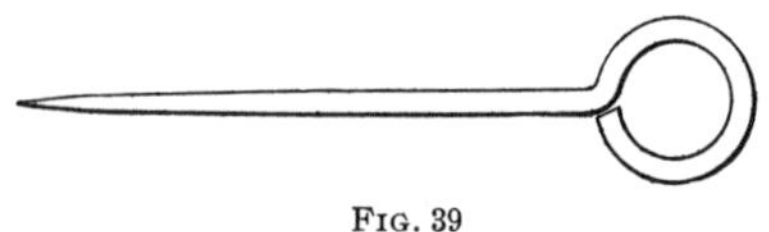

Fig. 39

55. Other Methods of Marking.—White lead or zinc white, mixed in naphtha or boiled linseed oil and applied with a slender brush, is often used to letter and number pieces of work, especially when shipped to a distance. Before laying out, the surface where lines are to be made may be whitened by rubbing with lump chalk or by coating with whiting and water, turpentine, or wood alcohol, which may be applied with a brush, and will dry quickly. When laying out work, the hand cold chisel and the center or prick punch are frequently used to locate the ends and intersections of lines marked on the piece of iron. Lines are often marked by a succession of dots made by the prick punch at intervals of from $\frac{1}{2}$ inch to 2 inches, according to the nature of the work.

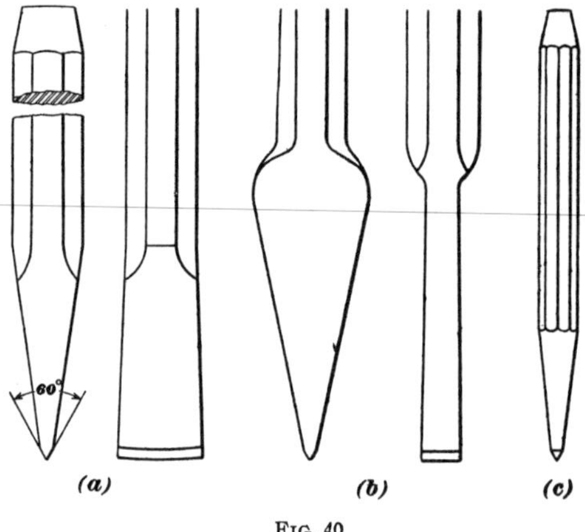

Fig. 40

56. Cold Chisel.—The cold chisel is usually of the form shown in Fig. 40 (*a*). A chisel about 1 inch in width and 7 or 8 inches long, made of $\frac{3}{4}$-inch octagon tool steel, is commonly used for general purposes. Small chisels are made of $\frac{5}{8}$ inch, or smaller, octagon steel. The illustration shows the edges formed by faces ground at an angle of 60°.

57. Cape Chisel.—The cape chisel shown in Fig. 40 (*b*) is used for cutting and trimming narrow grooves and slots, and is made in widths to correspond to the widths of the grooves to be cut. The length of the cutting edge should be slightly greater than the width of the tool behind it, to give clearance for the cut.

58. Center or Prick Punch.—The center, or prick, punch, shown in Fig. 40 (*c*), is made of the same material as the cold chisel. The size varies with the nature of the work, and may be from about $\frac{1}{4}$- to $\frac{5}{8}$-inch octagon steel. It is used to mark centers of holes to be drilled and to make small dots or marks wherever desired.

59. The Bevel.—A common form of bevel is shown in Fig. 41. The bevel is used to lay off angles other than right angles, and is usually set from a drawing or templet, or from a sample. It is sometimes called a **T** bevel, and often, incorrectly, a **bevel square.** The form illustrated has a cast-iron stock *a* with a slot in the middle of one end, through which slides a steel blade *b*, slotted for about one-half its length and capable of adjustment about a pivot in the end of the stock.

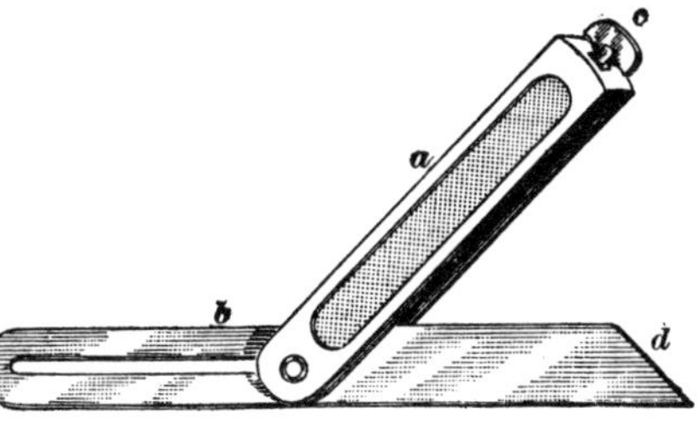

Fig. 41

The adjustment of the blade consists in varying the length of the projection of the blade *b* from either side of the stock, and of varying the angle that it makes with the stock. When the blade is set as desired, it is clamped by turning the thumb nut *c* on the end of the stock. The side edges of the blade are parallel and the solid end *d* is generally cut at an angle of 45°, or one-half a right angle, with the edges. Care must be taken not to tighten the thumb nut with more than a gentle pressure, otherwise the threads may be stripped from the screw. It is well to keep in mind, for use in checking up work, that the sum of the two angles formed by an edge of the blade with the sides of the stock is equal to two right angles. For testing angles while the work is hot, there is usually a shop-made bevel formed of two strips of steel, about $\frac{1}{8}$ or $\frac{3}{16}$ inch thick by $\frac{1}{2}$ or $\frac{3}{4}$ inch wide, and from 12 to 16 inches in length. These pieces are riveted together at one end and are made to work rather stiffly, so that they will remain wherever set.

60. Measures.—For measuring long rods, or bars, such as suspension rods and hangers, the more careful workmen generally use a steel measuring **tape.** For the general requirements of measuring small work, both straight and

FIG. 42

curved, a thin metal **rule,** 2 feet long by $\frac{3}{4}$ inch wide, folding in the middle, is commonly used. It is made either of a good quality of tempered spring steel or of hard-rolled brass. Fig. 42 illustrates the general form of this rule.

61. Hack Saws.—The **hack saw** is now usually considered a necessary part of the blacksmith-shop equipment. Hack-saw blades vary in length from 6 to 16 inches, and even longer, and may be used either in hand frames or in specially designed frames moved by power.

The hand frame illustrated in Fig. 43 (*a*) is an adjustable frame, in which blades from 8 to 12 inches long can be used. The clamps holding the blade may be turned so that the blade will cut up or down in the plane of the frame, or at right angles to the frame. Thus it is seen that the blade may be turned to face any one of four ways. Fig. 43 (*b*) shows the blade set at right angles to the plane of the frame.

Hack-saw blades are so hard that they cannot be filed, and are so cheap that when dull they may be thrown away. They are made with about 25 teeth per inch for sawing thin metal, and with about 14 teeth for other work. The blades used in hand frames are about $\frac{25}{1000}$ inch thick and $\frac{1}{2}$ inch wide, an 8-inch or 10-inch blade being the most economical. The operator should lift the frame up slightly when

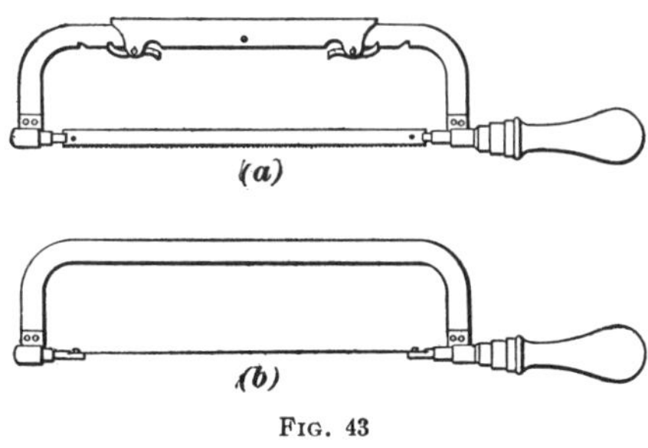

FIG. 43

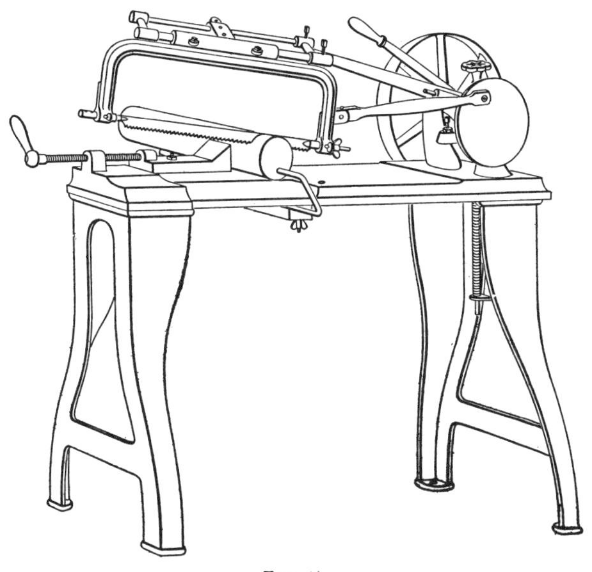
FIG. 44

drawing the saw back, or the back stroke, if the work is in contact with the teeth, will be much more destructive to the teeth than the forward stroke.

62. Power Hack Saw.—For cutting off bar stock, a **power hack saw,** like that shown in Fig. 44, will be found exceedingly useful. Such a machine is usually provided with a vise for holding the stock to be cut off, and is so constructed that the machine will stop when the piece has been sawed through. Provision is also made for lifting the saw on its back stroke so as to save the teeth. The blades are generally 12 inches or more in length, and will cut stock up to 4 inches in diameter. The power hack saw is especially useful for cutting off tool steel.

IRON FORGING

MANUFACTURE OF IRON

MAKING CAST IRON

1. Iron Ore.—Any iron-bearing mineral from which the metal can be abstracted at a profit is **iron ore.** This definition excludes many ores containing a large percentage of iron because they also contain a large percentage of impurities; and it will admit, on the other hand, many ores that carry a low percentage of iron, but few or no injurious elements. Iron is never found chemically pure in nature, except perhaps, in some meteorites, where it is a mere curiosity, while the limited supply from this source makes it of no practical value. Chemically pure iron is soft and ductile, has a high melting point, and can be forged and welded.

The *rich ores* of iron contain from 60 to 68 per cent. of metallic iron, while those low in iron, called *lean ores*, may contain only from 30 to 40 per cent. In the United States, very few furnaces are running on ore containing less than 50 per cent. of iron. The impurities, which consist of oxygen, silicon, phosphorus, lime, sulphur, magnesia, aluminum, manganese, titanium, etc., occur in very small amounts.

2. Blast Furnace.—Iron is reduced from its ores by fusing them, together with lime, in a **blast furnace;** the lime acts as a **flux,** and is obtained by the use of limestone and marble. A blast furnace is usually an iron shell lined with some refractory substance, such as firebrick or fireclay, and on the outside looks like a tall stack or chimney. Into it alternate layers of fuel, flux, and iron ore are thrown, the fuel fired, and the whole mass raised to a high temperature by means of an air blast, to hasten the combustion. The blast furnace is continuous in its operation; the ore, flux, and fuel are charged into the top of the furnace, and the ore and flux are melted by the intense heat and tapped out at the bottom. The amounts of fuel, limestone, and ore must be carefully calculated in order that the ore may be properly reduced. The furnace is so operated that the impurities in the fuel and ore may combine with the flux in the form of **slag,** which is lighter than the iron and floats on its surface. It is tapped from a hole at the side of the furnace, above the hearth or bottom, while the iron is tapped from a hole at the front and bottom of the furnace and flows into iron or sand molds where it cools. The form of cast iron obtained by this process is called **pig iron.**

3. Nature and Composition of Cast Iron.—The best and purest grades of **cast iron** are made in blast furnaces using charcoal for fuel. This is due to the fact that charcoal does not contain sulphur, while coal and coke do; and also because the ash is of such a nature that the impurities pass into the slag rather than into the iron. Cast iron, as made by blast furnaces, generally contains from 92 to 96 per cent. of metallic iron. The other 4 to 8 per cent. consists chiefly of impurities in the form of carbon, silicon, manganese, phosphorus, and sulphur, from 2 to 6 per cent. being carbon. While it is true that the five elements mentioned are impurities in iron, the first four are really the elements that make cast iron of commercial value. Cast iron has a granular or crystalline structure, and is hard and brittle. It can be cast in almost any desired shape, but cannot be forged or drawn into wire.

MAKING WROUGHT IRON

PUDDLING PROCESS

4. Nature and Composition.—Wrought iron has a fibrous structure and can be forged and welded. It is practically free from carbon, silicon, and the other elements contained in cast iron. It may be made direct from the ore, but the greater part is made from cast iron by the removal of its carbon, silicon, and other impurities, by the puddling process.

5. Hand Puddling.—In the manufacture of wrought iron by hand puddling, the cast iron obtained from the blast

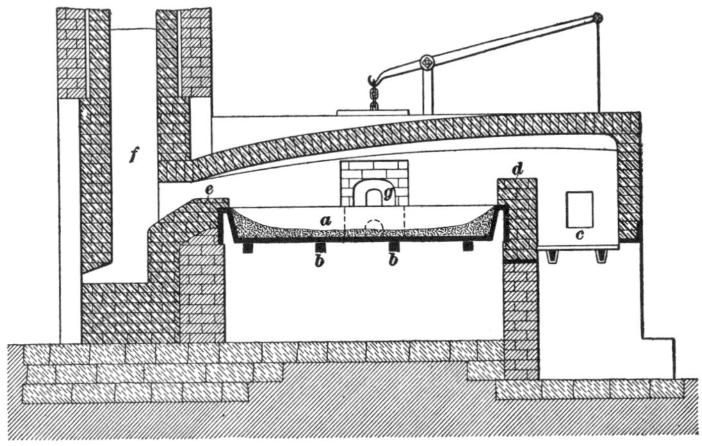

FIG. 1

furnace is melted on the hearth of an **open-hearth furnace,** which is ordinarily of the form shown in Fig. 1. The hearth *a* is usually made of cast-iron plates carried on brick walls or on iron supports *b*, *b*. It is generally about 5 or 6 feet in length and 4 feet in width opposite the charging door, and is lined with a refractory substance. The roof is a firebrick arch. The heat is obtained ordinarily from a bituminous-coal fire in the fireplace *c*. The area of the grate varies from 6 to 10 square feet or more, depending on the character of the iron, the draft. and the fuel. Between the grate and the hearth is a firebrick wall *d*, called a **bridge wall,** that extends across the furnace and is of sufficient height to keep the fuel from getting over on the hearth, and the molten iron from running over on the fuel. In many cases, the bottom and sides of the furnace are hollow, and have water circulating through them to keep them cool. Another bridge wall *e*, called the **altar,** prevents the metal from overflowing into the flue leading to the chimney *f*. In the middle of the door *g* in the side of the hearth is an opening large enough to admit the puddler's **rabble;** this is a long iron bar with which the melting charge of metal and slag is stirred by the workman.

The furnace is charged with 500 pounds of pig iron, which is carefully placed on the bed of the furnace or is broken up and piled around the sides. When the charge is melted, the puddler stirs the fluid mass with his rabble, while his assistant changes the draft and the fire to suit the different stages of the process. The impurities of the iron are taken up by the molten flux or burned out. In about an hour, pasty masses of metal begin to appear, which the puddler works into spongy balls weighing from 60 to 80 pounds each. These are well worked at a high temperature to get rid of the slag, and finally removed from the furnace and hammered or squeezed into the form called a **bloom.** The bloom is then taken to the rolling mill, and rolled into various commercial forms.

6. Mechanical Puddling.—In the various **puddling machines** in use the flame is led from the firebox to a hearth of varying form and construction, moved by machinery. In some forms this hearth is barrel-shaped and turns on a horizontal axis. In other forms it is circular, and is so arranged that it may be mounted on a vertical shaft and rotated; but in one form the hearth slants at an angle of from 10° to 15° from the horizontal. In most cases the metal is further stirred or mixed by broad-bladed rabbles operated by the workmen or by machinery.

The advantages claimed for these machines are that greater masses of metal may be handled and that there is greater uniformity of the product, together with a saving of fuel, time, and expense. Hand puddling is also injurious to the health of the workmen.

7. Effects of Reheating Wrought Iron.—It has been found by experiment that the strength of the puddled iron, as rolled into the bar, is increased each time it is heated and worked, up to about the sixth working. Each heating and working beyond this point decreases the strength, until at about the twelfth it will be as weak or weaker than after the first rolling from the puddled bar. Careless heating may, however, injure the iron in one or two heats.

FORGING OPERATIONS

DEFINITIONS

8. The operation of shaping or forming metal by hammering or pressing is termed **forging.**

The process of stretching a piece of metal in one or more directions, either by hammering or by pressure, is called **drawing.** In the blacksmith shop, the term always indicates a decrease in the area of cross-section of the piece, with a corresponding increase in its length or breadth.

By the term **bending** is usually meant the turning or forming of the iron in such a manner as to deflect it from a straight line. The finished product may be a curved or an angular piece.

In the operation of **twisting** an iron bar, the fibers are wound around each other spirally. No change in the direction of the axis of the piece takes place. Fig. 11 shows a hook that has the straight portion between the eye and the hook twisted.

Upsetting is the operation of increasing the thickness of a piece of iron by shortening it.

Forming refers particularly to the process of giving a desired form or shape to a piece of metal by hammering, or by means of specially formed dies between which or into which the metal is pressed or hammered.

Welding is the process of uniting two pieces of metal into one solid piece by heating them to a welding heat and hammering or pressing them together. For wrought iron, a white heat is necessary to soften the metal so that it will weld.

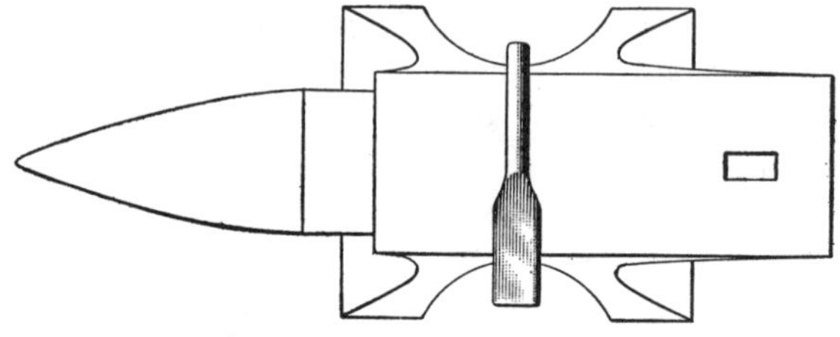

Fig. 2

EXAMPLES OF FORGING

DRAWING

9. Position of Work on Anvil.—In all work on the anvil, it must be remembered that the anvil is crowned crosswise, and the metal will therefore be drawn most readily in a direction at right angles to the length of the anvil. If the piece is to be drawn lengthwise, it should be laid across the anvil as shown in Fig. 2; if it is to be drawn sidewise, it

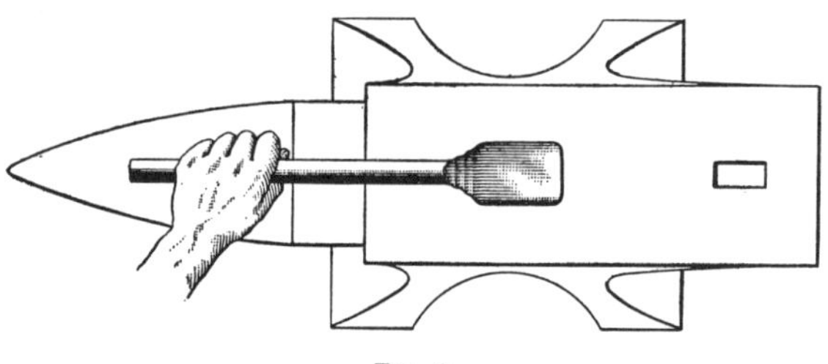

Fig. 3

should be held as shown in Fig. 3. The drawing may be done by holding the work across the horn of the anvil; the sharper curve causes the metal to flow more freely than on the face, but it is more liable to cause irregularities in the shape. When the work is to be straightened, it should be laid lengthwise, as shown in Fig. 3, because the anvil is straight in this direction.

FIG. 4

10. Round Drawing.—Drawing a bar of round iron out to a smaller diameter is one of the easiest forms of drawing. The portion to be drawn is marked with soapstone, and then heated carefully to the highest temperature it will stand without injury. It is then taken from the fire, quickly brought to the anvil, and hammered rapidly. The diameter may be reduced by two methods, first by keeping it as nearly round as possible during the entire process, and, second, by drawing it to a square, then to a round. By the first method, the piece is turned a little after each blow and kept as nearly round as possible, and finished with the hand hammer or with a swage, as shown in Fig. 4. A second heat is sometimes necessary. It is well to turn the piece from left to right and then from right to left, because turning it always in the same direction is liable to twist the fibers. By this method the iron is very liable to split. To avoid this, the second method is often preferred, the piece being drawn from a round to a square, then to an octagon, and finally finished to a round of the required diameter.

11. Square Drawing.—In round drawing, the iron is turned a very little at a time, so as to bring all points under

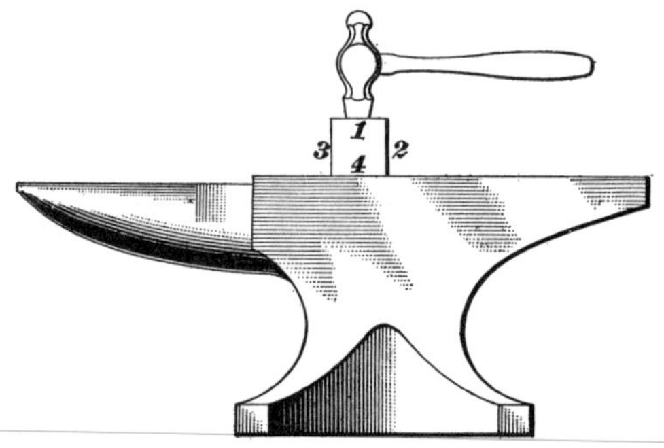

Fig. 5

the hammer. In square drawing, however, the iron must always be turned either one-quarter or half way around. This requires some practice, as the least variation in the amount of the turn will bring the piece out of square. In drawing a square bar down to one having a smaller section of the same shape, the sides of the original bar help to guide the hand in making the proper amount of turn, but if a round bar is to be drawn down to one square in section, the amount of turn must be entirely governed by the hand and the eye.

In drawing down a square bar to a square of smaller size, the piece is heated and brought to the anvil, holding one of the sides down flat and striking blows squarely on the top side, drawing it down along its entire length. It is then revolved one-quarter of a turn and the top side hammered until the piece is about square; the opposite side is then turned up and hammered; and finally the last side is brought under the hammer. The figures in Fig. 5 show the order in which the sides are brought under the hammer. This method of turning the work lessens the liability of getting the piece twisted, or diamond-shaped, as shown in Fig. 6.

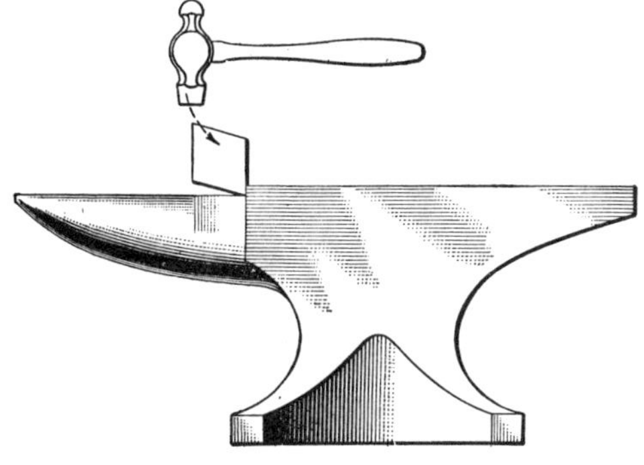

Fig. 6

If it becomes twisted in this way, it should be held as in Fig. 6 and struck in the direction shown.

If desired, the piece can be finished under the flatter; in this case it is held on the anvil lengthwise and the flatter held against the upper face parallel to the face of the anvil, while the helper strikes a few light blows.

BENDING

12. The character of the bending operations done on an anvil depends on the shape of the section of the piece to be worked—whether it is round, square, hexagonal, oblong, or of other shape—and on the size of the section. For instance, the operation of bending a square bar is very different from the operation of bending a wide but thin plate, having the same area of cross-section, to the same shape.

Small sizes of rods may be bent easily by placing them in the hardie hole, or the pritchel hole, of the anvil to the point at which the bend is desired, and bending the end over. Some pieces may be bent by doing the work entirely over the face of the anvil, whereas other pieces are bent over both the horn and the face of the anvil at various stages of the operation.

13. An Eye Hanger.—Suppose that it is desired to form the eye pipe hanger shown in Fig. 7, to support a pipe $1\frac{1}{4}$ inches in diameter; the eye is to be bent to the form shown, but not welded. A rod $\frac{1}{2}$ inch in diameter and slightly over 2 feet long is taken and marked at a distance of 6 inches from one end; this end is then heated to a bright red up to the point marked. The cool end of the rod is grasped with the left hand, and the marked point on the heated end is placed over the farther edge of the face of the anvil, or over the horn near its point. The heated end, which projects, is then bent down so that it points nearly at right angles to the rest of the rod. The rod is then turned on its axis half way around so that the heated end points up instead of down. The very end of the heated part is then brought down so that it projects slightly over the end of the horn, as shown in Fig. 8, and the end of the rod is bent gradually by light hammer blows into a ring as shown in Fig. 7.

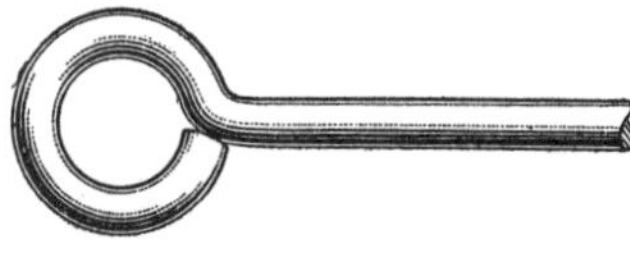

FIG. 7

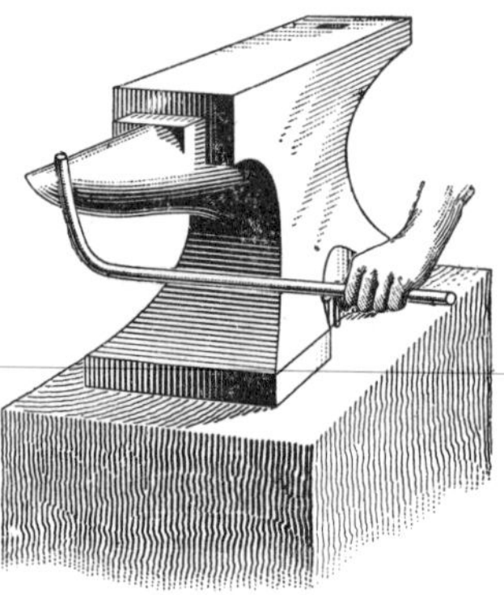

FIG. 8

14. Forging a Staple.—If a staple, like the one shown in Fig. 9, is to be made out of a piece of $\frac{1}{4}$-inch round iron, the required length is first marked off on the bar. On this, a distance of 1 inch from the end is marked off, and the end is heated and drawn to a square point $1\frac{3}{4}$ inches long. The piece is then cut off from the bar, using the hardie, as shown in Fig. 10, and making the piece $5\frac{1}{2}$ inches long, over all. The other end is marked and drawn out to a point the same as the first, keeping both squares in line. The piece will now be about $6\frac{1}{4}$ inches long, $\frac{1}{4}$ inch round in the middle, with a square tapering point $1\frac{3}{4}$ inches long at each end. The center of the piece is then marked and heated, and the piece bent over the horn of the anvil to the shape shown in Fig. 9, making the distance between the two straight, parallel ends $\frac{3}{4}$ inch. In bending over the horn of the anvil, the piece is held against the large part of the horn and bent

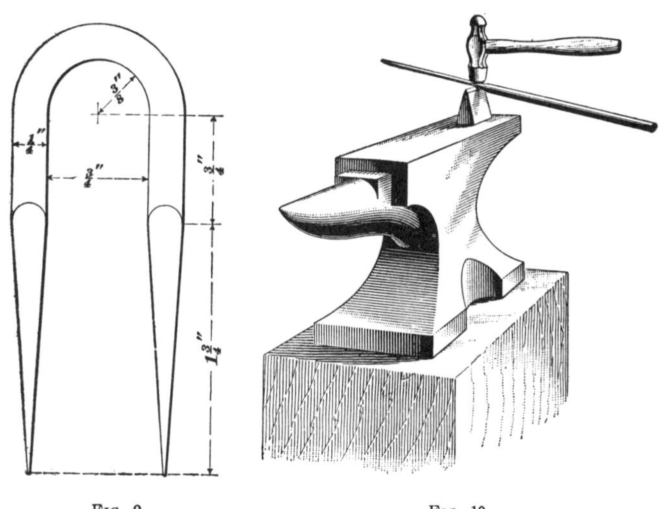

Fig. 9 Fig. 10

by light hammer blows, turning it to keep it round; then while hammering it the piece is gradually brought toward the point of the horn. When bent, the curve should be uniform and the two ends of the same length. If it is warped or twisted, it is flattened on the anvil with the hammer or the flatter.

TWISTING

15. Forging a Gate Hook.—If a hook, like the one shown in Fig. 11, is to be made of $\frac{1}{2}$-inch square iron, the operation will be about as follows: It will take about 4 inches of stock to make the hook, and this length is marked off from the end. It is then heated and drawn out until it calipers $\frac{3}{8}$ inch square, when it will be about $5\frac{1}{2}$ inches long. A length of $1\frac{3}{4}$ inches is then marked off from the end and drawn to a round of $\frac{5}{16}$ inch diameter, keeping one side straight, as shown at *d*, Fig. 12.

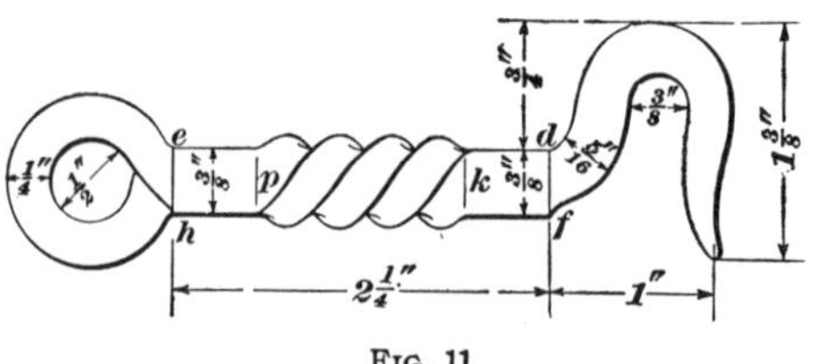

FIG. 11

The shoulder, or offset, *f* is formed over the edge of the anvil, as shown in Fig. 13. By striking the upper edge with the hammer, as shown, the top will remain straight at *d*,

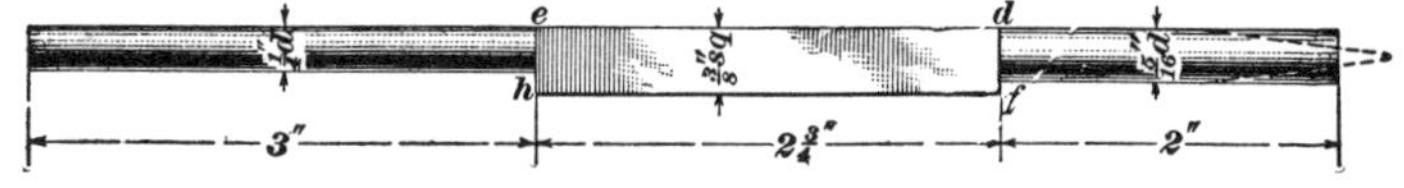

FIG. 12

after which it can be finished with the swage to make it perfectly round. A length of $\frac{3}{4}$ inch is then marked off on the $\frac{5}{16}$-inch end and the point drawn down round, as indicated by the dotted lines, Fig. 12. The entire piece is then cut off from the bar and the other end of the $\frac{3}{8}$-inch square marked off, making the distance between the shoulders $2\frac{3}{4}$ inches, and drawn to $\frac{1}{4}$ inch round, as shown in Fig. 12, keeping it straight at *e* and forming a shoulder at *h*.

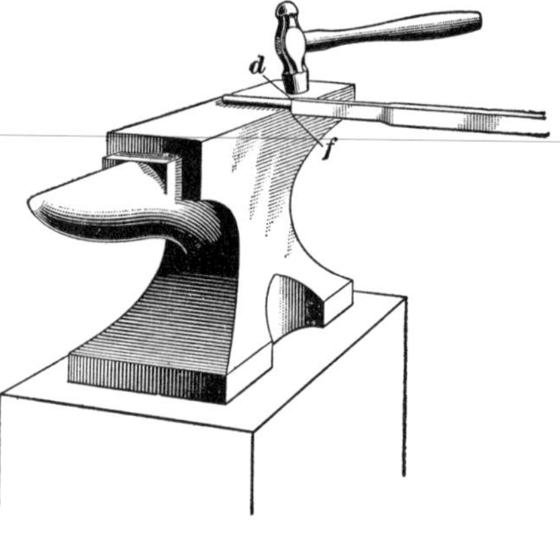

FIG. 13

The $\frac{1}{4}$-inch round part is bent into a ring over the horn and the $\frac{5}{16}$-inch round end is bent into the hook, as shown in Fig. 15. In bending the hook and the ring, the

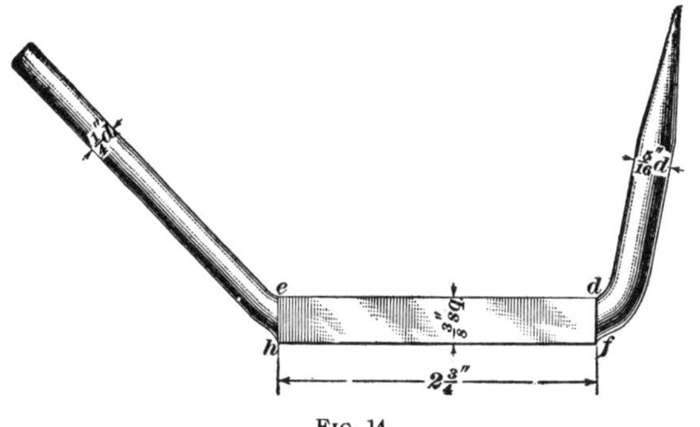

Fig. 14

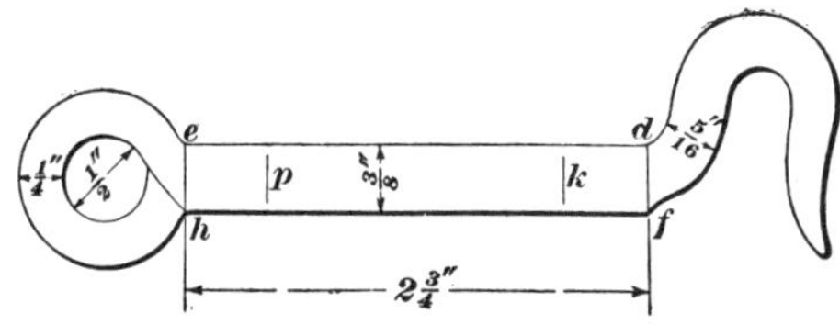

Fig. 15

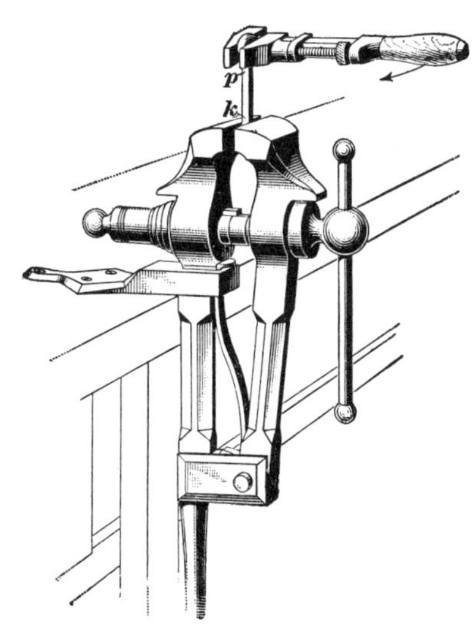

Fig. 16

piece is held with one round end projecting over the farther edge of the anvil, and this projecting end is bent back until it has the shape shown in Fig. 14. The other end is then bent in this way, and the ring and hook formed over the horn of the anvil by light hammer blows.

16. Twisting the Hook.—Lengths of $\frac{1}{2}$ inch are now marked off on the square part from the shoulders *f* and *h*, giving the points *k* and *p*, Fig. 15. The portion between *k* and *p* is then brought to an even red heat and twisted. To do this, the piece is clamped vertically in the vise by the hook end, as shown in Fig. 16, with the point *k* at the top edge of the vise jaw, and a monkeywrench is fitted to the ring end, immediately above the point *p*. The wrench is then given one complete turn, twisting the square part as shown in Fig. 11. If it has become bent, it may be straightened by hammering it between two blocks of wood on the anvil so as to avoid battering the sharp edges.

UPSETTING

17. Ramming.—When it is desired to **upset,** or thicken, a portion of a piece of iron, this part is heated to a bright red, the rest of the bar being kept cool by pouring water over it with the sprinkler. When sufficiently heated, the piece is brought to the anvil and upset, either by ramming or with the hammer.

If the bar is from 2 to 3 feet long and is to be upset at the end, the heated end of the bar is rammed against the face of the anvil, as shown in Fig. 17, or on a block of iron bedded in the ground, called a **bumping block.** The entire energy of the blow is concentrated at the hot end of the rod, and drives the particles of the iron near the end together in the direction of the blow; this bulges out the iron where it is hot.

18. Upsetting With a Hammer.—If the bar is short, it may be brought to the anvil with a pair of tongs, as shown in Fig. 18, and held vertically on the anvil with the hot end up and the heated end hammered, or with the hot end down and the blows struck on top of the cold end. By the second method, the heated end is constantly in contact with the cold face of the anvil and will therefore cool very rapidly; the result is that the bar will not spread so much on the end

FIG. 17

but the bulge will extend up a little farther than by the other method. In the same manner an upset may be made at any point on the bar.

19. Precautions in Upsetting.—If, in upsetting a bar, it begins to bend after a few blows have been struck, the piece must be straightened at once, for any blows struck endwise on a bent bar will not have much effect in upsetting it, but will only bend the bar more and make the straightening harder. For upsetting, a good heat is required; in fact, it is well to make the final heat a welding heat, because upsetting often separates some of the fibers, and by taking a welding

FIG. 18

heat over the piece and hammering it on the sides a little, all loose fibers will be welded together again.

MAKING A BOLT

20. Square-Headed Bolt.—If a ½-inch bolt, Fig. 19, is to be made out of a ½-inch round rod, the end of the rod is heated and upset. When enough metal has been upset to form the head, the enlarged end is reheated and the cold end of the bar passed through a suitable hole in the swage block, or through the heading tool. If the latter is used, it is laid on the anvil so that the body of the bolt passes

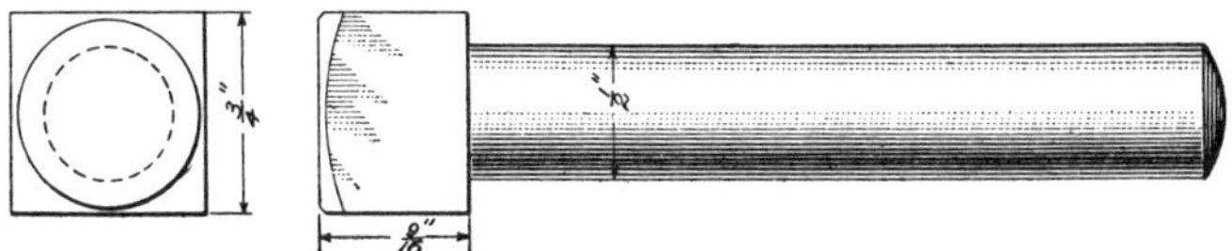

Fig. 19

through the hardie hole. The upset end is then hammered down against the swage block or heading tool, as shown in Fig. 20, until the head is $\frac{9}{16}$ inch thick, and the piece driven out of the heading tool. The head is then shaped

Fig. 20

square with a hand hammer. If, after the sides of the head are properly formed, it is found that the head is longer than it should be, it is laid on a piece of soft iron placed on the anvil and the extra length cut off with the hot cutter. After this, the bolt is put back into the heading tool and the head is finished with the hammer; the bolt is then cut off to the desired length, and the **burrs,** or rough edges, on the end are hammered down.

21. Bolt Header.—When a large number of bolts are to be made, it is well to use a **bolt header,** one form of which is shown in Fig. 21. The frame is of cast iron and quite heavy; steel dies are provided for bolts of different sizes, usually varying by $\frac{1}{8}$ inch, although occasionally $\frac{7}{16}$-inch and $\frac{9}{16}$-inch dies are used. The length of the bolt is determined by a steel block *a* provided with notches that engage a series of notches on the frame of the machine. This block may be set for any length of bolt within its range. The iron may be cut to length so as to leave the right amount of stock to make the head without any trimming. The dies are closed to grip the iron by means of the foot treadle *b* and the head formed with a hammer. The dies fit in the top of the machine at *c*, the two dies forming a heading tool.

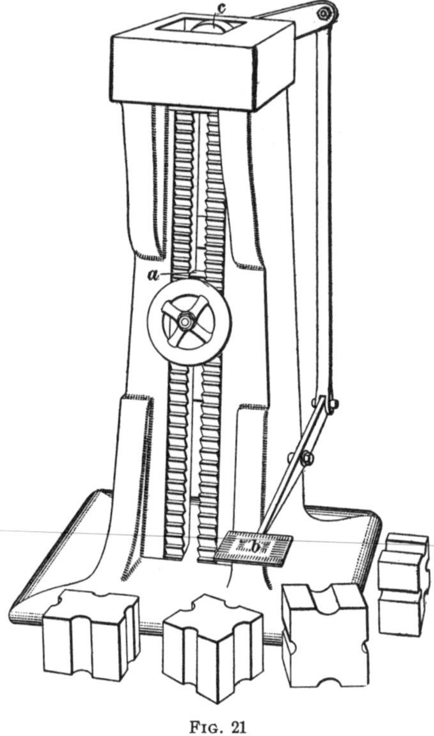

Fig. 21

22. T-Headed Planer Bolt.—The method of making a T-headed planer bolt is as follows: Suppose that the bolt is to be made from a $\frac{5}{8}$-inch round rod; the size and form of the head for the bolt are shown in Fig. 22, indicated by the dimensions and letters of the top and side views. The points *a b c d* of the head in the top view correspond to the points *a′ b′ c′ d′* in the side view. First the shape of the head is made oblong in cross-section, as indicated in the top view by the letters *a e c f*, and $\frac{3}{8}$ inch thick. The end of the rod is then heated and upset; but the upsetting is not a continuous operation; it must alternate with hammer work to keep the sides *a f* and *e c* parallel. For the latter, the bolt is laid flat on the face of the anvil with first one side *e c* placed uppermost to receive the blows of the hammer, and then the opposite side. Also, the head is frequently moved beyond the edge of the anvil and is struck with the hammer for the purpose of both forming and upsetting it. This process of upsetting and forming is continued until the amount of metal upset is sufficient to form the desired head. This is then heated and the cold end of the rod is passed through the right size of hole in a swage block, or through a heading tool, and the inside face of the head is worked to shape. But this latter cannot be done at one operation, for the side faces, shown in the top view at *a e* and *c f*, must be brought to shape with the hammer. The final shape of the head shown in the top view by *a e c f* is obtained by dressing the side faces *a e*, *e c*, *c f*, and *f a* and the end face of the head with the hammer, and by finishing the inside face on the swage or heading tool. The lengths *e b* and *f d*, each equal to $\frac{1}{4}$ inch, are marked off with a soapstone pencil or a hand chisel and the portions of the head *a e b* and *c f d* are then cut off with the hot cutter. The angles *b a d* and *b c d* are approximately equal to 65°, and hence if the bevel is used it may be set to this angle and used to test the angles between the faces. It is not desirable that the edges at *a* and *c* be made sharp. The head of the

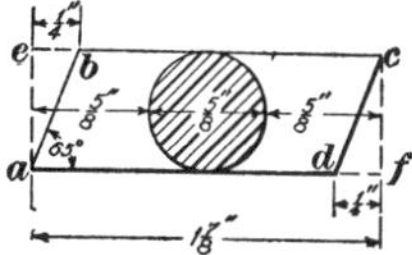

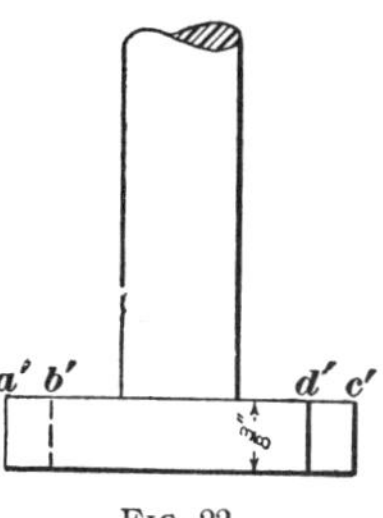

Fig. 22

bolt is made thin so that it will break off before the pressure becomes great enough to injure the lip of the **T** slot on the cast-iron planer table. The head of the bolt is given the shape shown in Fig. 22 so that it will not turn in the **T** slot, when the nut is tightened. After the head is properly formed, the bolt is cut to the required length.

23. Making a Hexagonal Bolt Head.—If it is desired to form a hexagonal, or six-sided, head on a $\frac{3}{4}$-inch bolt of

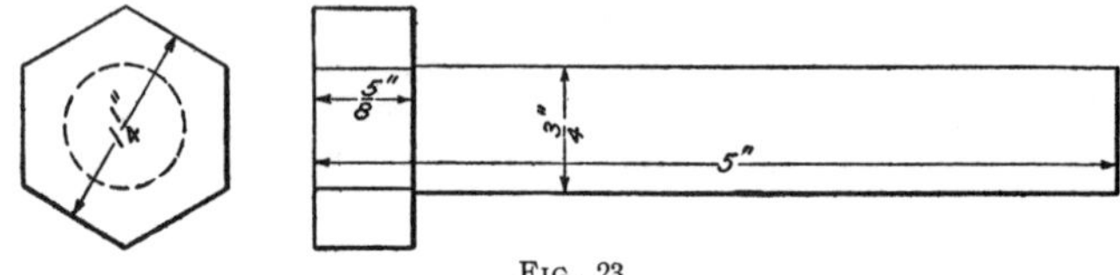

Fig. 23

the dimensions shown in Fig. 23, the end of a $\frac{3}{4}$-inch round rod is heated and upset. When enough metal has been upset to form the head, the cold end of the bar is passed through a suitable hole in the swage block or the heading tool, and the inside face of the head is surfaced around the shank of the bolt as described for a square-headed bolt.

The head is then shaped in a three-sided groove of proper size, which is usually formed on the surface of the swage block. The swage block is placed so that the groove is horizontal and the opening is on top. The inside face of the head is trued up, as before, and the side faces are again touched up with the swage, after which the head, if it is too long, is marked for the proper thickness and the end cut off with the hot cutter. A hand hammer is also used in the final dressing of the head. A cup-shaped swage may be used for finishing the top of the head into the rounded shape shown in Fig. 24.

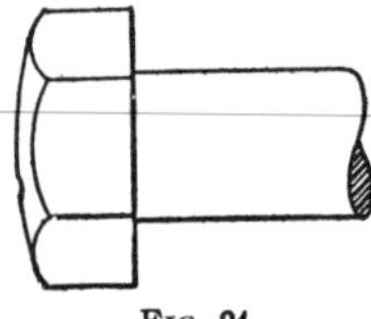

Fig. 24

The bolt is finally cut to the proper length, which in this case is 5 inches, and the burrs on the edges dressed down with the hammer.

24. Stock for Bolts.—Iron bolts can be made from bars of the same diameter as the diameter of the bolt, the heads being made by welding on rings or by upsetting the stock. Steel bolts must be made from bars as large or larger than the head, and the body drawn down to the required size.

MAKING AN ANGLE

25. If an **angle**, like the one shown in Fig. 25, is to be made from a bar of $\frac{3}{8}$-inch square iron, it will be necessary

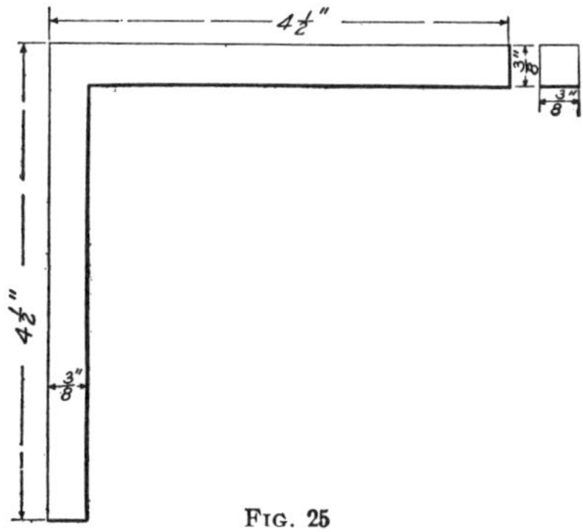

Fig. 25

to upset the bar in the center to give the additional stock required for the corner. About $8\frac{3}{4}$ inches of stock is cut off, and the center heated and upset to $\frac{5}{8}$ inch diameter, as shown in Fig. 26. The piece is then bent at right angles in the center by sticking one end through the hardie hole down to

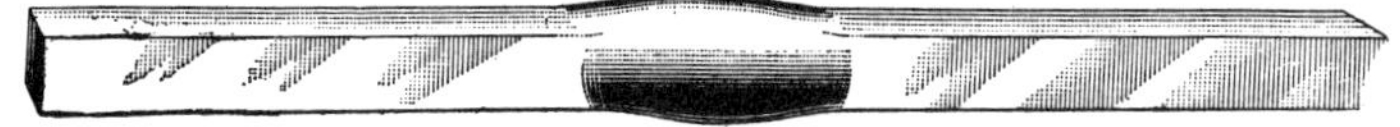

Fig. 26

the heated center and bending the other end toward the anvil, as shown in Fig. 27. To make the corner sharp, the piece is held on the face of the anvil, as shown in Fig. 28, and the angle made true by hammering. When striking the blows the hammer is drawn as shown by the arrow in Fig. 28; this draws the iron toward the corner. The piece is finished $\frac{3}{8}$ inch square with the flatter, and the ends cut to an equal length on the hardie, and then squared with the hammer.

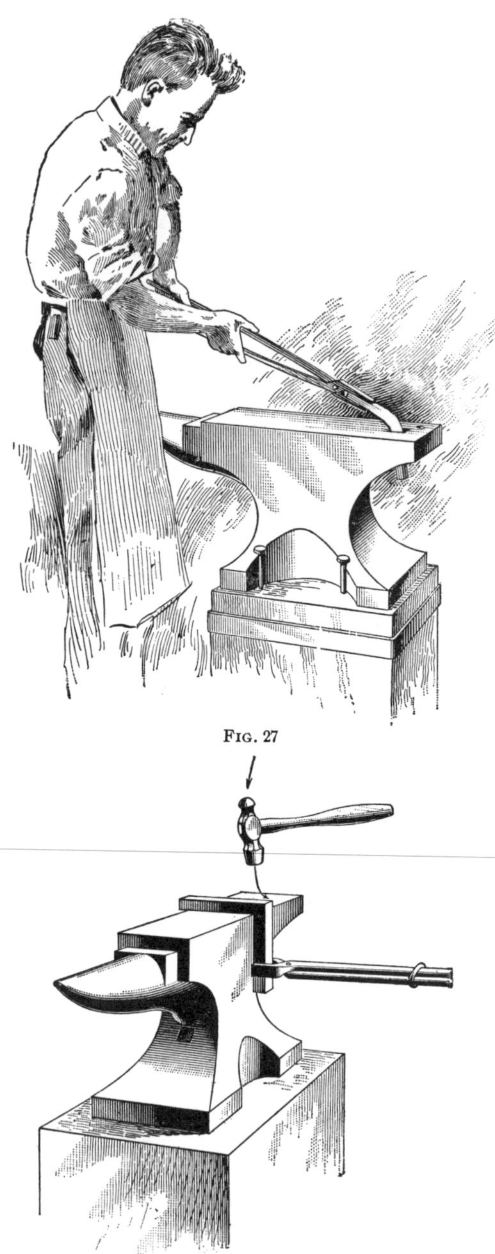

Fig. 27

Fig. 28

MAKING A SMALL CHAIN HOOK

26. If the chain hook, shown in Fig. 29, is to be made from a bar of $\frac{1}{2}$-inch round iron, about $6\frac{1}{2}$ inches of stock is required. The end will have to be upset to provide stock for the eye of the hook. To provide enough stock to make the eye, a length of $1\frac{1}{2}$ inches is marked off from the end of a bar, and the end heated and upset as shown in Fig. 18, until the original $1\frac{1}{2}$ inch length is shortened to 1 inch. The piece is then flattened down to $\frac{3}{8}$ inch in thickness, making the upset portion circular and about 1 inch in diameter, as shown in Fig. 30.

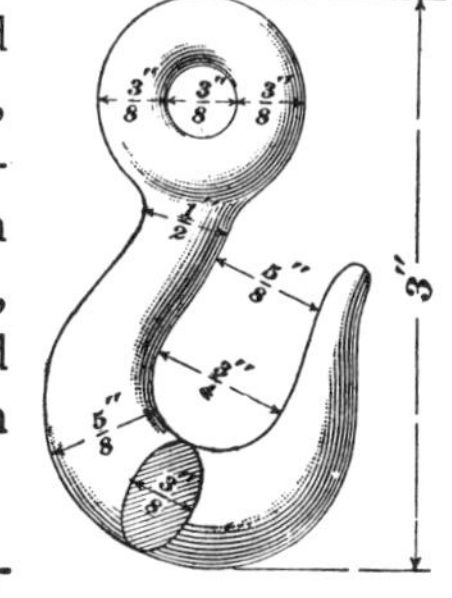

FIG. 29

27. Forming the Eye.—In flattening the upset portion down to $\frac{3}{8}$ inch in thickness, it should be spread sidewise as much as possible. If it draws out in length, it may be upset a little in a swage or heading tool, or it may be upset on the edge of the anvil as shown in Fig. 31. When the head has been formed, it is heated, and a $\frac{1}{4}$-inch hole put through with the punch, which should be kept cold by dipping it in water before and after

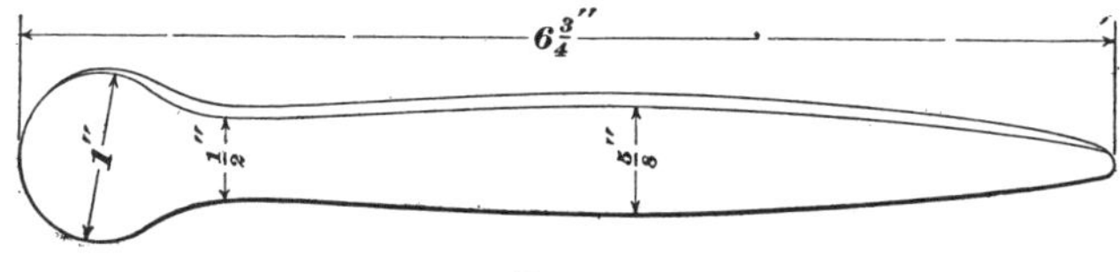

FIG. 30

it is used. After the hole is started, the punch is held aside to see whether it is in the center; if it is, the punch is driven down well and the piece is turned over and punched from the other side, where the iron shows a black circular spot. The core is driven out through the hardie hole or through the pritchel hole. Some smiths put a little coal or coke dust into the hole after it has been started and then finish the hole by driving the punch on top of it; this keeps the point of the punch cool and prevents it from sticking in the hole.

When the hole has been punched, the eye of the hook is raised to a welding heat and worked over to weld up any parted fibers or split places. For this, the punch is put into the hole and left there while hammering the eye. The punch is driven down occasionally to keep it tight; this will spread the hole to about $\frac{3}{8}$ inch in diameter.

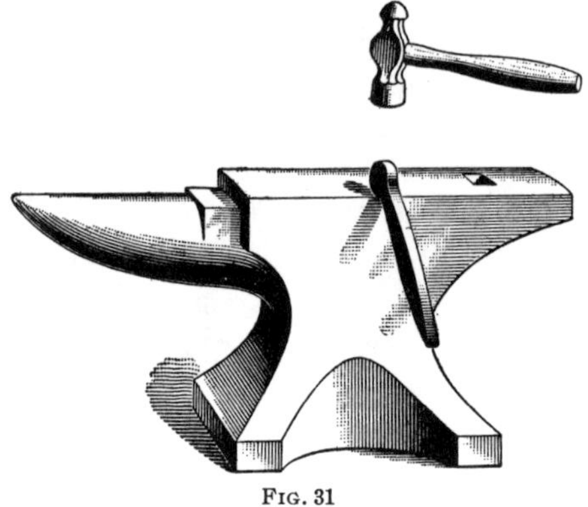

FIG. 31

Another method of making the eye is to take a sufficient length of material to form the eye of the hook by bending the end of the rod around a pin, a mandrel, or the end of the horn of the anvil. The eye end of the rod is first scarfed as shown at *a*, Fig. 32 (*a*), and is bent around to form the eye as shown in Fig. 32 (*b*), after which the end is welded. These latter operations will be described in detail under separate headings in connection with welding operations.

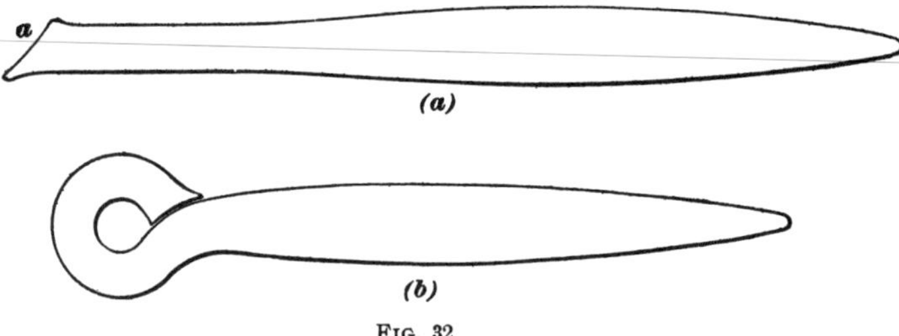

FIG. 32

28. Bending the Hook.—The corners are next rounded and the hook bent into the required shape by holding it on the horn of the anvil and striking it with a light hammer.

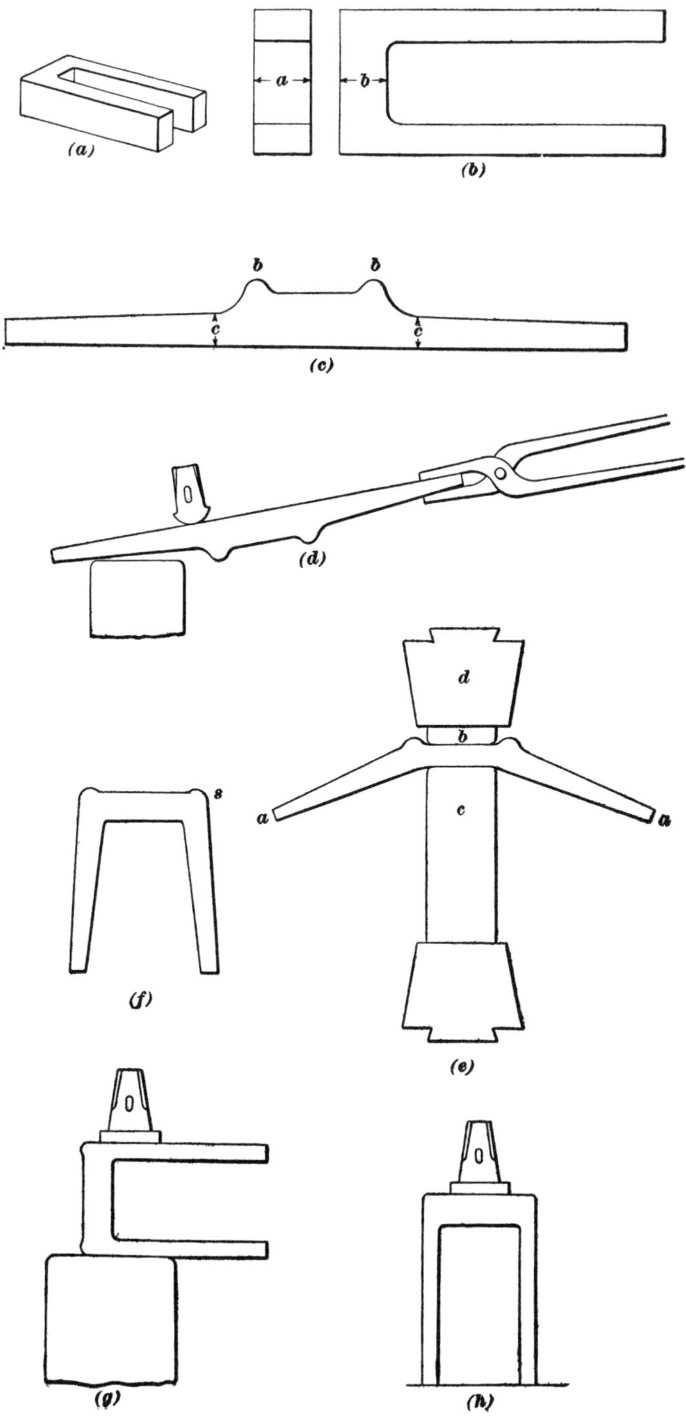

FIG. 33

FORGING ROD STRAPS

29. Forging a Strap to Size.—To make a rod strap of the form shown in Fig. 33 (*a*), select stock of the width shown at *a* in Fig. 33 (*b*), and thicker than *b* by a sufficient amount to form the corners *b* in Fig. 33 (*c*). Draw this stock to the form shown in Fig. 33 (*c*), leaving the sides slightly thicker at *c* than they will be in the finished strap, as they will draw in the bending, and being careful that the hammer leaves no ridges, which would tend to start cracks, sometimes called **gaulds,** in the corners, which become

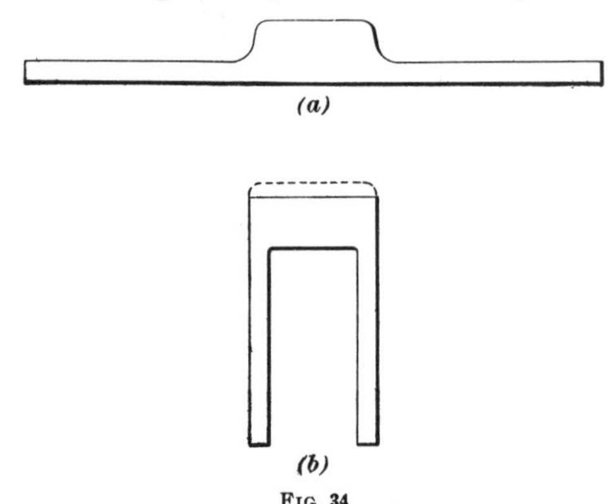

FIG. 34

deeper as the work progresses. Next, take the stock in the tongs, and, holding it as shown in Fig. 33 (*d*), proceed to bend it, using a large fuller to start the bend, as by starting in this way the iron is not cramped at the corners. Any ridges left by the hammer may be taken out by the fuller when starting the bend.

After the bends have been started as shown in Fig. 33 (*d*), place the stock in clamps, or hold it in the steam hammer in the manner shown in Fig. 33 (*e*). This may be done by lowering the upper die *d* on the upper one of two blocks *b* and *c*, between which the stock is held, and holding it firmly by means of the steam pressure. Next, have two helpers, one on each side, strike simultaneously on the ends until the piece has the form shown in Fig. 33 (*f*). Take a heat on one corner by placing the side *s* down in the fire; and by using the flatter, bring the side to the shape shown in Fig. 33 (*g*), and repeat this on the other corner and side. It will be necessary during this operation to use the flatter on the strap, which is held as shown in Fig. 33 (*h*), in order to make the end of the proper shape.

30. Forging a Strap and Trimming to Size. Another way to make this strap is to use wider stock and forge it to the form shown in Fig. 34 (*a*). The sides are then bent in the same manner as in the operation just described, and the strap brought to shape as before. The end is formed, however, by cutting off the excess of stock that has been allowed there, as shown by the dotted line in Fig. 34 (*b*).

WELDING

CONDITIONS GOVERNING WELDING

31. Object of Welding.—It is often necessary to join together two pieces of iron, or the ends of the same piece, so that the joint will form one solid mass. In such cases, the pieces are **welded** together.

Each of the pieces treated thus far has been made of a single piece of iron, but very frequently it would be inconvenient or impracticable to make the forging out of one piece. If so, several pieces are welded together, and the forging is said to be **built up.**

32. Oxidation of Iron.—If a piece of iron is heated in air, it will absorb oxygen from the air, thus forming a **scale** of oxide of iron on the surface. The hotter the iron, the more rapidly the scale will form. It does not adhere to the iron very firmly, and surfaces coated with it cannot be welded. It is therefore very important to guard against oxidation of the surface of the iron if a weld is to be made, because the scale of oxide will lie between the two surfaces of the iron and prevent their coming in contact; and under these conditions it will not squeeze out if the pieces are pressed and hammered together. Two methods are employed to guard against the oxidation; namely, the use of a *reducing fire* in heating, and the use of suitable *fluxes*. By both of these methods the hot iron is prevented from coming in contact with the oxygen of the air.

33. Reducing Fire.—A **reducing fire** is one in which all oxygen is consumed in the combustion, so that the gases coming in contact with the iron do not contain any oxygen that can unite with the iron. Under this condition no oxidation can take place, and the surface of the iron will remain clean. This condition is obtained in a closed fire by having a thick bed of fire for the air to pass through before coming in contact with the iron and by maintaining a moderate blast. If, however, the blast passes through a thin bed of fuel or if more air is blown through than the fire needs, the unused oxygen will oxidize the iron. Therefore, a thick fire should always be maintained, and the blast regulated so as to supply just enough air and not too much.

34. Fluxes.—The other method for preventing the oxidation is to coat the surface of the iron with some substance that will exclude the air. It must, of course, contain no oxygen that will unite with the iron. It must be fluid at a heat below the welding heat of iron and still not become so fluid at the welding heat that it will run off and leave the iron exposed as before.

Substances used for preventing the formation of scale on the iron when being heated for welding are called **fluxes.** Strictly speaking, most of them form a fusible mixture with the iron oxide, which offers the desired protection to the iron, but they use up some of the iron to make this mixture, therefore wasting it. This mixture, however, is so liquid that it will squeeze out from between the surfaces being welded, thus leaving clean surfaces of iron to be welded together. There are many kinds of fluxes. Some of these consist of a mixture of several substances. The most common flux for wrought iron is clean, sharp sand; this fuses readily on the surface of the iron and sticks to it during the heat, thus excluding the air. A very good flux for iron, but one that cannot be used on steel because it tends to reduce the carbon, can be made by mixing 2 ounces of calcined borax and 1 ounce of sal ammoniac. **Calcined borax** is a good flux for steel. It is made by heating borax in an iron pot until the water is driven off. The mass is then cooled and pulverized. Calcined borax is also called *borax glass*.

Sand and borax are very good fluxes for iron alone; but it is well to have a flux that can be used when welding steel to iron. A very good flux for welding steel to iron is made of potter's clay, wet with strong brine. This is dried and powdered and used like sand or borax. Another good flux that is not too fluid, and does not injure steel, is made by mixing 3 ounces of carbonate of potash, also called pearlash, with 1 ounce of dry clay. This is heated in an iron pot, and when hot, 4 ounces of calcined borax is added. When cold, it is powdered, and is then ready for use.

CLASSIFICATION OF WELDS

35. Names of Welds.—The different kinds of welds are named according to the manner in which the pieces are put

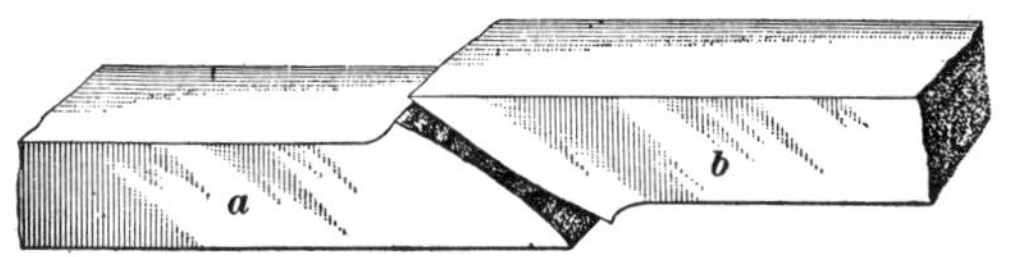

FIG. 35

together; the principal ones are *scarf welds*, *butt welds*, *lap welds*, *cleft welds*, and *jump welds*. The selection of the weld to use depends on the form of the piece, the forces it is to resist, and the equipment for making the weld.

36. Scarf Welding.—In the scarf weld, the two pieces are *scarfed;* that is, they are thinned down, as shown in the pieces *a* and *b*, Fig. 35. If the iron is of uniform thickness, it is first upset at the point at which the weld is to be made in order to gain a little in thickness; after this, it is scarfed.

To do this, the upset end is thinned down, generally with the peen of the hammer, drawing it out thin at the point and crowding the metal back at the stock by drawing the hammer as shown at *a*, Fig. 36. Sometimes the end of a flat bar, after being upset, is tapered or scarfed by using a fuller, as shown in Fig. 37. This is a quick and effective way of doing it. The faces to be welded should be rounded and made higher at the center, as shown at *b*, Fig. 36, so that the pieces first come in contact at this point, in order to give the slag and impurities an opportunity to squeeze out as the weld is being closed.

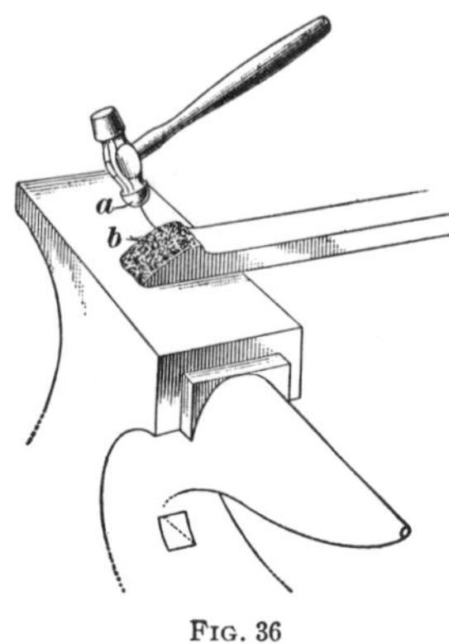

FIG. 36

The scarfed ends of both pieces having been brought to a welding heat, and fluxed if necessary, the weld is made as follows: Holding the shorter piece with the tongs in the right hand and the longer piece in the left, the scarfed faces of both being downwards in the fire, draw both out of the fire and give each a sharp rap on the edge of the anvil to remove any coal or other substance that may adhere to the heated surfaces. Next bring the shorter piece to the position on the anvil shown at *a*, Fig. 38 (*a*), and follow with the longer piece, bringing it to the position of the dotted outline *b*; then, without losing contact between the longer piece and anvil, bring *b* down on *a*, as shown in Fig. 38 (*b*). The

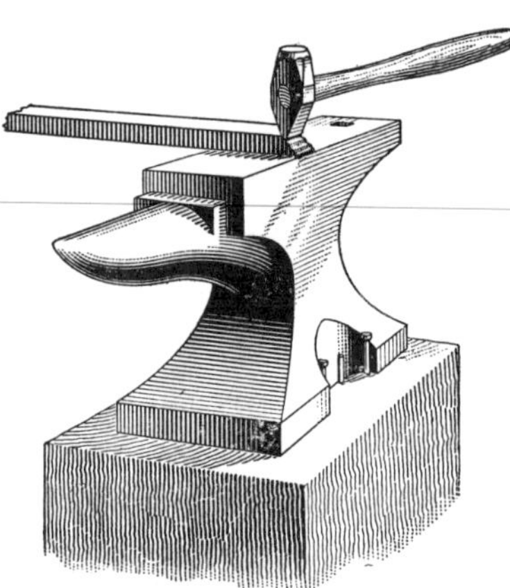

FIG. 37

contact of *b* with the anvil assists in controlling its movements. When *b* is placed on *a*, a slight pressure on it will hold both in relative positions while the tongs are dropped and the right hand relieved so that the hammer may be taken and a light blow delivered in the direction of the arrow *c*, Fig. 38 (*b*). As soon as the pieces stick together, the ends of the scarf may be brought down by delivering a few light blows on one side, and then the piece turned over and the other side struck in the same manner before it has cooled below the welding heat. If the scarfs are made too long, it increases the surface to be welded and entails useless labor.

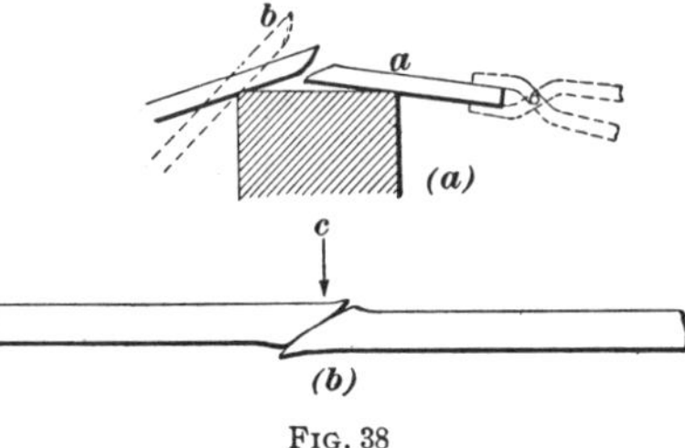

Fig. 38

37. Butt Welding.—In the butt weld shown in Fig. 39, the two pieces are generally upset a little at first, and then welded together as shown. They are hammered on the end to bring them together, and as this tends to upset the pieces still more, they are drawn out to the required size after the weld has been made. In preparing the ends, the surfaces to be welded are made convex, as in the scarf weld, in order to allow the slag to work out.

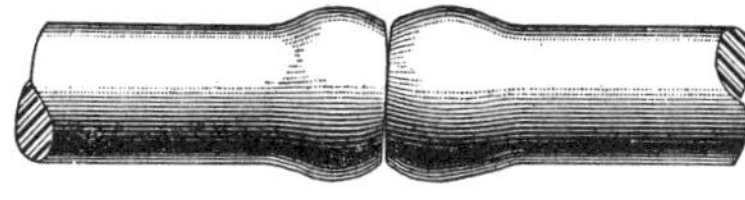
Fig. 39

38. Lap Welding. In the lap weld, the two pieces are laid together face to face, as shown in Fig. 40, and welded. As the faces are not rounded, the hammering is started at the center, gradually working toward the edges in order to work out all the slag. If the edges are welded up and any slag remains between the faces, it will keep the metal from uniting in the center.

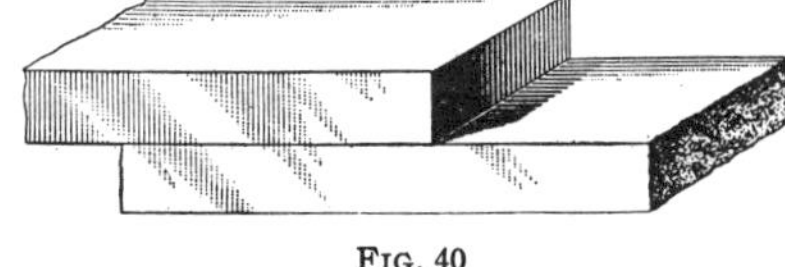
Fig. 40

39. Cleft Welding.—When a weld is required to stand considerable strain, such as is caused by prying and bending, the pieces are generally joined by the **cleft weld**, shown in Fig. 41. One of the pieces *a* is upset to gain width and thickness, and is then split open on the end, as shown at *a*, and the two cheeks *c* and *d* spread apart; the other piece is then scarfed on both edges, as shown at *b*. In welding, the pieces are first hammered on end to get the weld to stick, and then hammered on the edges to close the weld. The pieces should be so formed that the weld will start at the point *f* and the slag be forced out as the sides *c* and *d* are closed down.

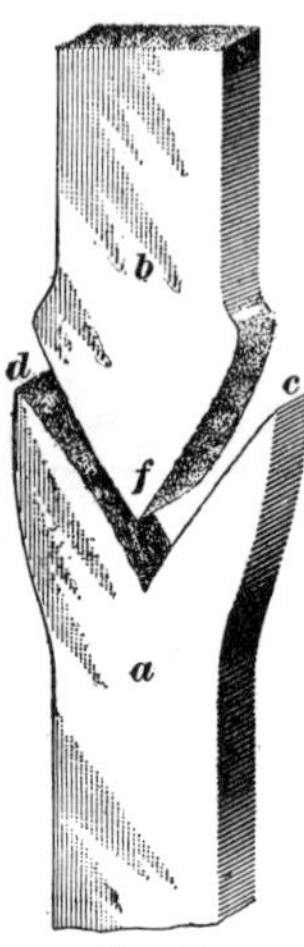

FIG. 41

40. Jump Welding.—The jump weld is really a special form of cleft weld. If it is desired to weld a bar to a flat plate, a conical depression is made in the plate as shown at *a*, Fig. 42. The bar to be welded is pointed as shown at *b*. The two conical surfaces must be so formed that the parts will come together at the point first, so that any slag will be squeezed out as the piece is driven, or jumped, into its seat. This form of weld is frequently used for quite large work, the bar being driven to place under the steam hammer.

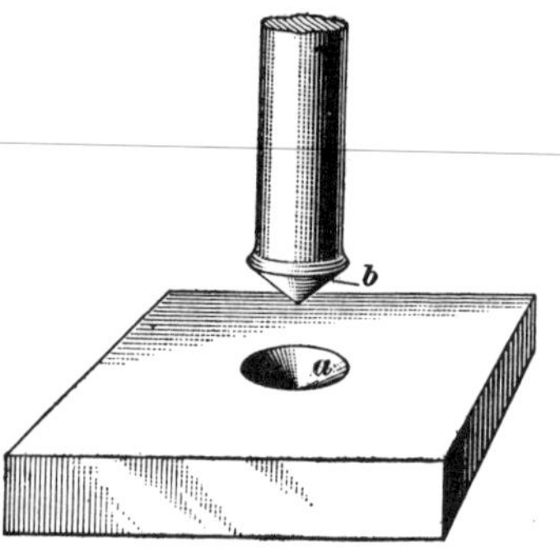

FIG. 42

41. Building Up.—It is frequently inconvenient or impracticable to make a forging out of a single piece because of the shape it is to have. In such a case the forging is built up; that is, it is made of a number of pieces that are forged to their approximate shapes and then welded together. Fig. 43 shows a built-up forging in which the welds are designated by the letters *a*, *a*.

42. Fagoting.—The operation of welding a quantity of wrought iron in small pieces, as scrap iron into a slab or billet, is called **fagoting,** and sometimes **shingling.**

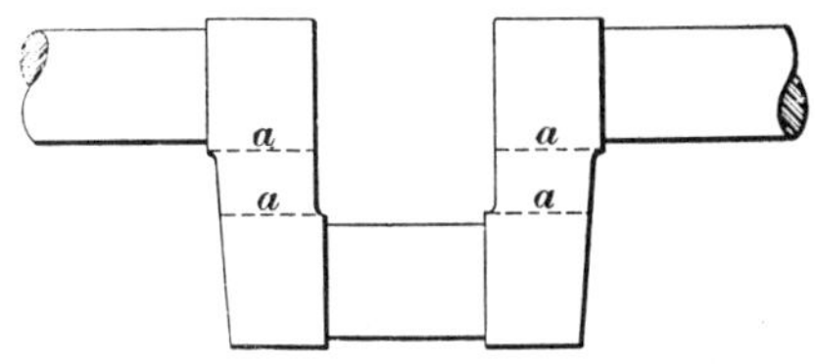

Fig. 43

In fagoting, a flat piece of iron is laid on a board and the pieces of scrap iron are piled on top of it, making a firm rectangular pile with large pieces around the outside and small pieces in the center; or, the flat piece on the board may be omitted, as shown in Fig. 44. The

Fig. 44

pile is then heated in a furnace and welded under a steam, or other suitable, hammer.

WORK INVOLVING SCARF WELDS

43. Making a Corner Plate.—In order to illustrate some of the applications of the **scarf weld,** a few simple cases, in addition to the one already given, involving the various principles of welding in general and of scarf welding in particular, will be described.

If a corner plate, like the one shown in Fig. 45 (*a*), is to be made, two pieces of $\frac{3}{8}'' \times 1\frac{1}{4}''$ iron, each about 15 inches long, are heated at one end, keeping one of them near the edge of the fire so as to heat it more slowly than the other. When one is hot enough, it is taken from the fire, and the end upset and then scarfed, as shown in Fig. 45 (*b*). This is done by striking it, and at the same time drawing the hammer toward the hand, as shown in Fig. 36, in order to draw the metal that way. The other piece

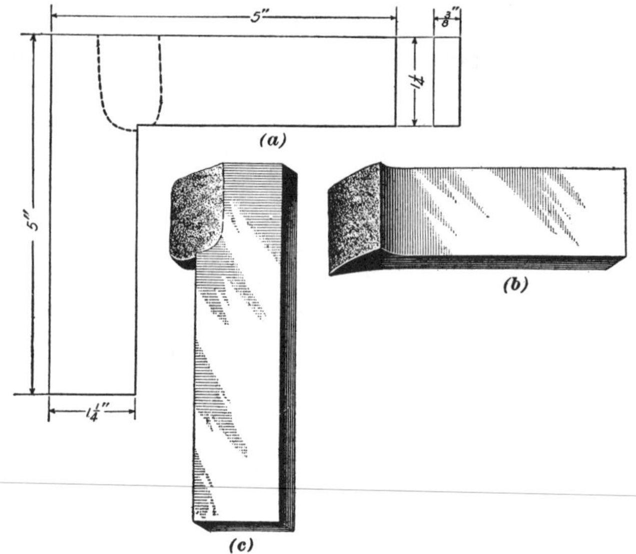

FIG. 45

is then taken from the fire, upset at the end, and one edge scarfed as shown in Fig. 45 (*c*). When both pieces are ready, they are put into the fire and raised to a bright-red heat, turning them occasionally to get the heat even. They are then dipped into the flux or the flux is sprinkled over their surfaces and they are then returned to the fire and raised to a good white heat on the *scarfs*. The pieces are turned occasionally to prevent the slag and flux from dropping off. As soon as both pieces begin to approach a welding heat, the blast is turned on stronger in order to raise the final heat rapidly; and if it is thought necessary, a little more flux is thrown on the pieces while in the fire. When hot enough, the pieces are brought to the anvil and put together. In doing this, the pieces are held against the edges of the anvil, somewhat as in Fig. 38, care being taken not to touch the cold anvil with the heated portion. When the scarfs are in line, the pieces are brought down flush on the anvil, having the piece in the right hand below the one in the left hand, so that the left-hand piece will be able to hold the other down while the right hand does the hammering. A few rapid blows will make the pieces stick; they are then turned over to bring the other face under the hammer.

The form of the scarf should always be such that the centers of the surfaces to be welded come in contact first; this will cause the slag to squeeze out as the pieces are hammered together. As soon as the pieces cool to a cherry red, they are reheated and the weld finished. When black hot, both sides of the piece are struck against the horn to make sure that the weld is well made. A good weld will not open on being bent and then straightened. If the weld is good, the corner is tried with a try-square and finished perfectly sharp and square, on the edge of the anvil, as shown in Fig. 45 (*a*). The ends are then cut off, making each arm 5 inches on the long edge. When cold, it will be seen that the weld is perfectly tight, the slag having all been squeezed out in hammering.

44. Making a T Plate.—A T plate like the one shown in Fig. 46 (*a*) can be made in nearly the same way as the piece described in Art. **43.** The cross-piece *a* is upset in the center and the edge is scarfed as shown in Fig. 46 (*b*), and the piece *b* is upset and scarfed on one end, as in the corner plate. When both pieces have been prepared, they are heated, fluxed, and welded, as described in the construction of the corner plate.

45. Making a Band Ring.—In making a band ring, like the one shown in Fig. 47 (*a*), a piece of $\frac{3}{8}'' \times 1\frac{1}{4}''$ iron,

12 inches long, is upset at both ends. The ends are scarfed on opposite sides, as shown at *a* and *b*, Fig. 47 (*b*), and the iron is bent into the form of the desired ring. To do this,

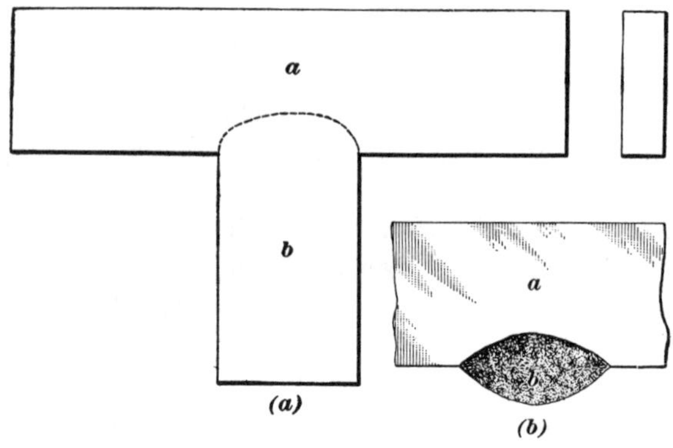

FIG. 46

the iron is heated and then laid across the horn of the anvil and projecting beyond it. The projecting end is hammered and bent around, as shown in Fig. 47 (*c*), until the scarfed

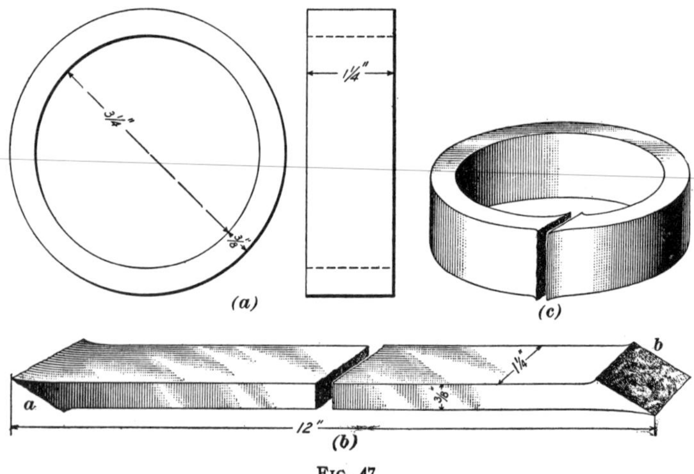

FIG. 47

faces are in position for welding, but about $\frac{1}{4}$ inch apart. The ends are next heated and fluxed, and then raised to a welding heat. To weld the ring, it is brought to the anvil and slipped over the horn, with the scarfed ends on the upper side of the horn. A few rapid blows with the hammer will make the weld, after which the ring is trued up so as to make it round and to make the iron of the required width and thickness throughout. This is done over the horn of the anvil.

A very good way of bending the iron for a band ring, or a similar piece, is to use a piece of ½-inch or ¾-inch round iron bent into **U** shape, as shown in Fig. 48 (*a*). This piece is clamped in the vise with the open end up, and the iron to be bent is laid between the projecting ends and bent by pressing the end sidewise, as shown in Fig. 48 (*b*), or a fork that has a square shank to fit the hardie hole of the anvil, as shown in Fig. 48 (*c*), may be used. The iron may be bent either hot or cold. If the iron is thin, it is preferable to bend it cold, as hot bending is liable to kink it. If thin iron is bent hot over the horn of the anvil, the jarring from the hammer blows is also apt to make the projecting end sag and lose its shape.

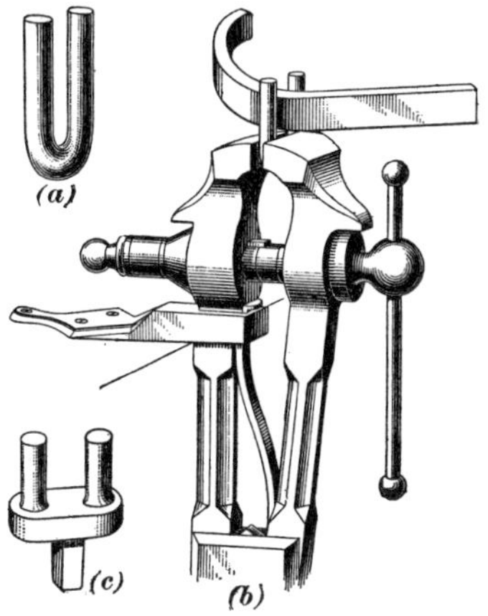

FIG. 48

46. Length of Stock for a Ring.—The following rule will be found convenient for determining the amount of stock required for either band or round rings.

Rule.—*Add together the inside diameter of the ring and the thickness of the stock and multiply the sum by* $3\frac{1}{7}$.

EXAMPLE.—What is the length of stock necessary for a ring of 2-inch round iron having an inside diameter of 12 inches?

SOLUTION.— $12 + 2 = 14$; $14 \times 3\frac{1}{7} = 44$ in. Ans.

To this must be added a small amount for upsetting and scarfing; in this case from ⅛ to ¼ in. should be allowed.

47. Making a Ring Hook.—A ring hook of the form shown in Fig. 49 (*a*) may be scarf-welded. It also shows, in its construction, a method of splitting stock for branch pieces that is valuable in smithing operations. On a piece of iron

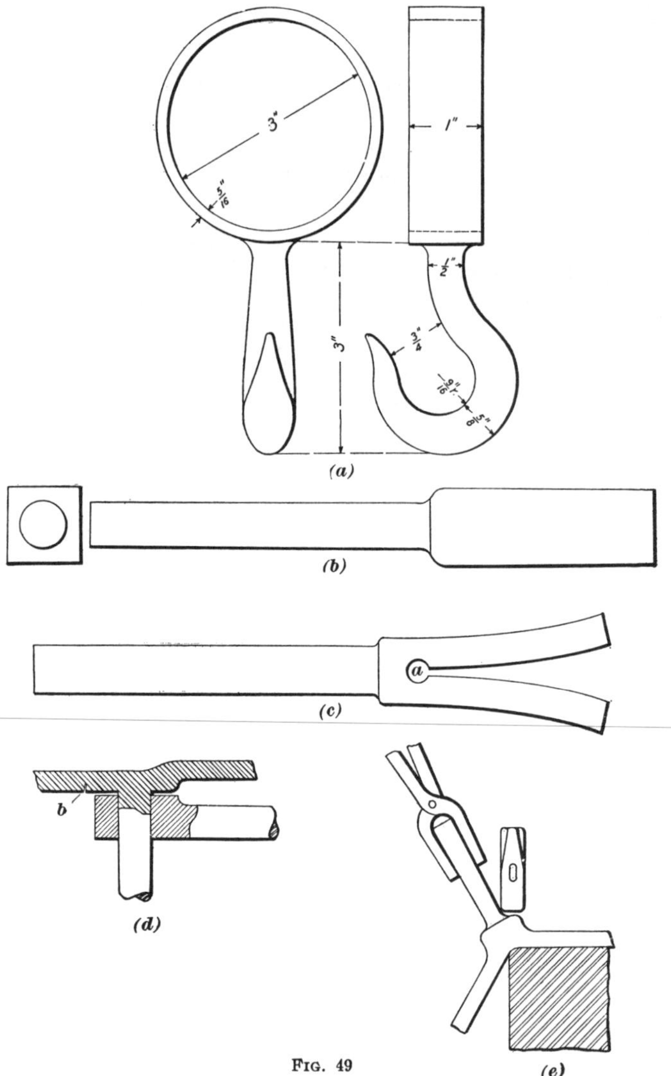

Fig. 49

of good quality, such as Norway iron, $\frac{7}{8}$ inch square and 5 inches long, mark off with a center punch 2 inches from one end and draw this piece out to 5 inches, leaving the stock of the form shown in Fig. 49 (*b*). Next, the hole shown at *a* in Fig. 49 (*c*) is made with a punch, the stock split out to the end, and the branches bent apart, as shown. The shank is then placed in a heading tool and the branches bent out, as shown in Fig. 49 (*d*). During this part of the work, great care must be taken to prevent cracks from starting in the corners, as shown at *b* in Fig. 49 (*d*). When the iron has closed around cracks started in this way, they are known as **cold shuts,** and the piece is liable to be dangerously weak where they occur. They may be avoided by removing the piece from the heading tool when the branches have been partially bent out, placing it over the round corner of

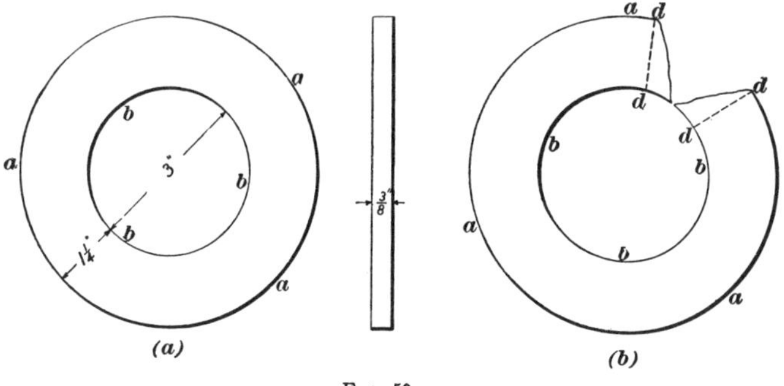

FIG. 50

the anvil, and using a large fuller or a set hammer in the manner indicated in Fig. 49 (*e*). The branches are drawn out to the proper dimensions, scarfed, bent to the ring form, and welded as in the case of the band ring. The piece is held in the tongs by the ring while the hook is being shaped. The finished piece should be sound, show no scarf or weld marks, and agree with the dimensions of the drawing.

48. Making a Flat Ring.—In making a flat ring, as shown in Fig. 50 (*a*), a piece of $\frac{3}{8}'' \times 1\frac{1}{4}''$ flat iron 14 inches long, is cut off and heated, and the end farthest from the tongs is bent edgewise over the horn of the anvil. As the circumference of the outside circle *a a a* of the ring is considerably greater than the circumference of the inner circle *b b b*, the iron will be upset along the inner edge and stretched along the outer edge by the bending. This will make the iron thicker than $\frac{3}{8}$ inch at the inner edge and thinner along the outer; the iron will also buckle and twist when being bent. By hammering it flat on the anvil, using the flatter if desired, the iron can be brought back to an even thickness; however, it should not be allowed to get far out of size, and its width and thickness should be frequently tried with the calipers. When bent, the iron will have the form shown in Fig. 50 (*b*); the corners are then cut off as shown by the dotted lines *d*, *d*, the ends scarfed and the iron bent on the anvil, as shown in Fig. 51, until the scarfs overlap, their inner surfaces remaining about $\frac{1}{4}$ inch apart, as shown in Fig. 52. The heat is then raised, the weld made, and the ring finished with the hammer.

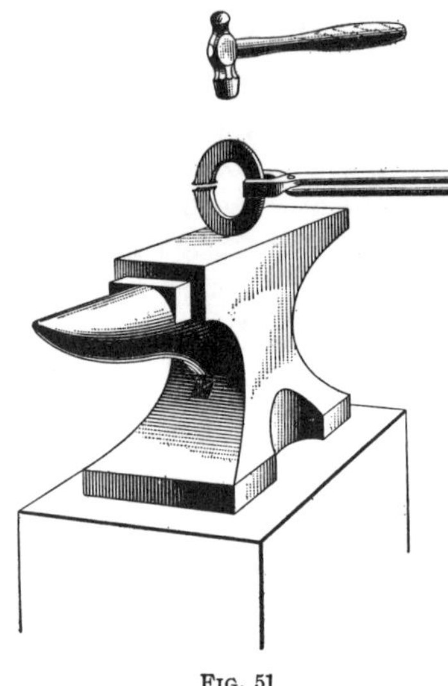

FIG. 51

49. Making a Small Chain.—In making a chain like the one shown in Fig. 53 (*a*), six distances of $3\frac{1}{2}$ inches each are marked off on a bar of $\frac{1}{4}$-inch round iron, 29 inches long. These marks may be put on with a soapstone pencil or the rod may be nicked on the hardie. One end of the rod is then heated, scarfed, and bent to the shape shown in Fig. 53 (*b*); it is then cut off obliquely at the first mark, as shown by the line *a a′*; this makes only a single scarf necessary on each weld. This link is then heated, fluxed, and welded, and bent into the proper shape. By the time the first link is finished, the next section of the rod is hot

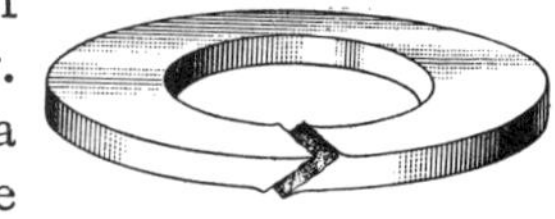

FIG. 52

enough to scarf and bend into shape. The rod being cut off at an angle makes it easy to scarf, but the hammer must be drawn, as shown in Fig. 36, in order to crowd up the iron at the large end of the scarf. When the second link is ready to weld, it is fluxed and the heat raised. When at a welding heat, the link is brought to the anvil, the first link caught up in it, and the weld made, or the previous link may be caught up in it after fluxing and before putting it into the fire for the final heat. In this way, five links can be made, the heat for scarfing and bending a link being raised while the previous link is being welded. The sixth link joins the other five links to the chain hook. After the

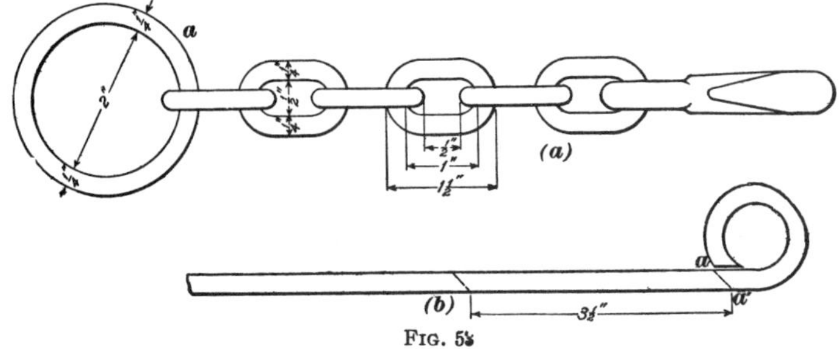

FIG. 53

sixth link is approximately bent into shape, the fifth link of the chain and the hook are caught up by it; its ends are then brought into proper position and are heated and welded. It is often of advantage to both the maker and user to have the hook link made slightly longer than the others.

When the six links of the chain have been made, the ring shown at *a*, Fig. 53 (*a*), can be made of the remaining 7 or 8 inches of the rod. The iron is scarfed at one end and bent into shape, after which the first link is picked up in the ring, which is then heated and welded. The chain can be finished by brushing it with a stiff brush and some sand and water, after which it is heated to a dull red and dipped into linseed oil or rubbed with a piece of oily waste, guarding carefully against fire in case the oil ignites.

50. Making a Pair of Tongs.—To make a pair of blacksmith's tongs for holding flat iron, such as is shown in

Fig. 54, a bar of $\frac{3}{4}$-inch square iron, not more than 2 feet long, is marked at 2 inches from the end and heated. When hot, the marked end is flattened to a thickness of $\frac{7}{16}$ inch, leaving the shoulder, as shown at *a*, Fig. 55 (*a*), on one side. This may be done by holding the iron so that the marked edge is on the edge of the anvil and by flattening

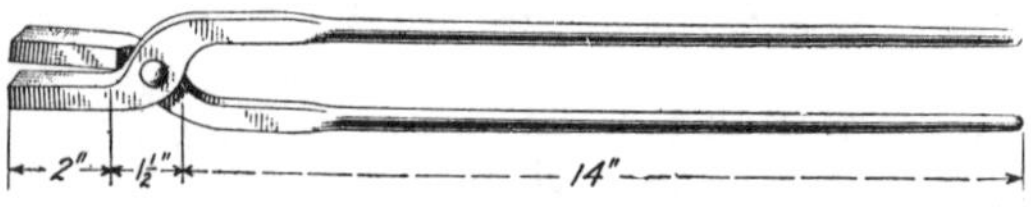

FIG. 54

the end with the hammer as shown. The piece is again heated and placed on the anvil, as shown in Fig. 55 (*b*), and flattened for about 3 inches in length. It is then cut from the bar and the other end *cg* of the piece is offset, as shown at *c*, Fig. 55 (*c*), and flattened for about 3 inches in length. The end *gd* is then drawn down to $\frac{1}{2}$-inch round, as is shown in Fig. 55 (*c*). The end *d* may be left a little

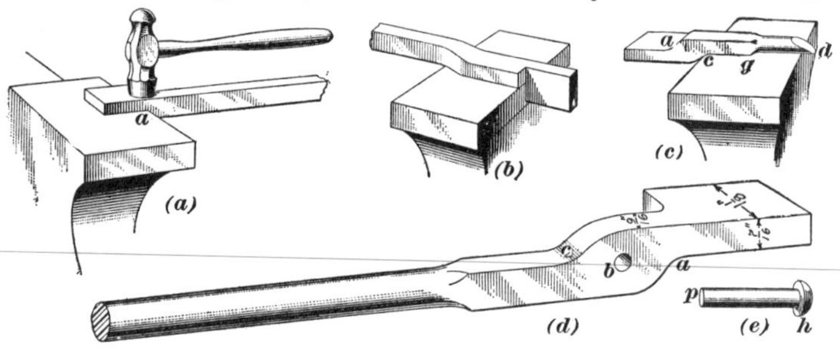

FIG. 55

larger than $\frac{1}{2}$ inch, and then scarfed for welding. Another piece is then made like this, and a $\frac{1}{2}$-inch round rod 12 inches long is welded to each to form the handles. A $\frac{3}{8}$-inch hole is then punched through one of the pieces, as shown at *b*, Fig. 55 (*d*). The two parts of the tongs are now held together and the hole marked in the second piece by punching it through the hole already made. The first piece is then laid aside and the hole punched through the other one.

The pin or rivet, shown in Fig. 55 (*e*), that is to hold the two parts together is made by upsetting a $\frac{3}{8}$-inch rod at one end and forming it into a head. It is then cut from the bar, making it the proper length, and tried in the tongs to make sure that it fits. The pin is then put into the fire and heated on the end *p*. When hot the finished head *h* is cooled by being dipped into the water, but the end *p* is left hot. The pin is then put back into the fire and heated on the end. When hot, it is put through the two holes and the tongs finished by riveting the end of the pin. It frequently happens that the rivet bends in the holes; this makes the tongs tight, but the jaws will not stay parallel. In such a case the rivet is driven out while it is still hot and another one made.

The fuller may be used to good advantage in making the tongs. The bar having been cut down part way with the hot cutter, the material may be worked out to approximately the correct form with the fuller. Sometimes, it is well to *take a heat over* the work; this consists of going over the piece, when it is at a white heat, with a light hand hammer. In this way, the fibers that have become separated are rewelded and the forging improved.

In making tongs, it is well to inspect the parts very closely before putting them together. A good way to detect flaws and defects is to heat the suspected part to a dull red; this will show all defects such as cracks, seams, poor welds, etc. The welds, angles, offsets in the jaws, and the metal near the punched holes are very liable to show defects. If the defects cannot be remedied, a new part must be made.

WORK INVOLVING BUTT WELDS

51. Knuckle-Joint Strap.—To make a knuckle-joint strap, shown in Fig. 56 (*a*), a short bar of stock is taken, slightly wider than one-half the width *a* of the strap, and of the thickness shown at *b*. The notch *c*, Fig. 56 (*b*), is made with the fuller, and the end of the bar drawn to the form shown by the dotted lines. Next, this end of the bar is cut off at such a place as will give the piece shown in Fig. 56 (*c*), and the face hollowed as shown at *d*. A second piece of the same form is then made, except that the face *d* is convex instead of concave. There will now be two pieces, as shown in Fig. 56 (*d*); these are to be welded together, the excess of width having been given, that they might close slightly at *f*, Fig. 56 (*d*), during this operation.

To weld them together, the two pieces are heated at the same time. When at a welding heat, the pieces are placed on the anvil in the relative position shown in Fig. 56 (*d*), and the weld made with light blows of sledge hammers, or they may be placed between the dies of a power hammer and welded with light blows, care being taken that the blows do not draw the sides too close to each other. Too heavy blows

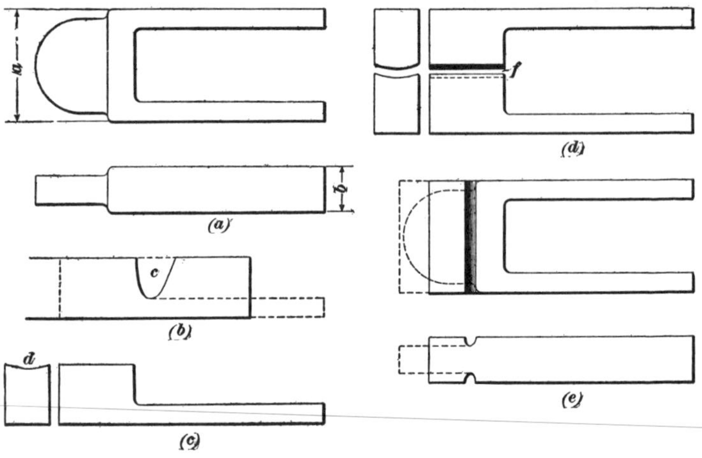

Fig. 56

are liable, also, to spread the edges of the weld and weaken it. The piece should be turned on its side, after the faces are welded, and the sides closed before the welding heat is lost. It must be remembered that the weld is due to the fluid condition of the metal at the surfaces that are joined, and the blows delivered should have only force enough to bring the surfaces entirely together. After the weld is made, the grooves shown at Fig. 56 (*e*) are made with the fuller, and the end drawn out as shown by the dotted lines. The end is then cut to the curved form shown in Fig. 56 (*a*) by the use of a hot cutter, and this end finished on the anvil.

WORK INVOLVING LAP WELDS

52. Making a Bolt Head by Welding on a Ring.—In this example, it is required to form the head of the bolt by welding a ring around the end of a round rod $1\frac{1}{4}$ inches in diameter. Fig. 57 (*a*) shows the form and dimensions of the bolt to be made. The ring should be made from a piece of bar iron 1 inch wide and $\frac{1}{2}$ inch thick. The length of the stock required may be found by the rule already given. The diameter of the ring, $1\frac{1}{4}$ inches, and the thickness of one side, $\frac{1}{2}$ inch, are added together, giving $1\frac{3}{4}$ inches. Then, $1\frac{3}{4} \times 3\frac{1}{7} = \frac{7}{4} \times \frac{22}{7} = 5\frac{1}{2}$ inches, which is the length of

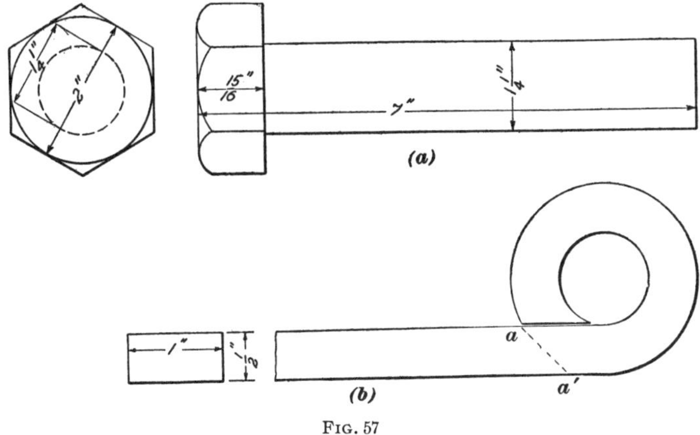

FIG. 57

stock required for the head. The end of this piece is upset slightly and scarfed, and then bent around, as shown in Fig. 57 (*b*); it is then cut from the bar by an oblique cut *a a'*. The ring and the end of the rod are then heated and fluxed for welding. When taken from the fire, the end of the rod is quickly placed in the ring and they are welded together by light hammer blows on the side of the ring. For this operation, the position of the rod is horizontal, and it is turned so that the hammer may strike different portions of the side of the ring at each blow. Care should be taken that the ends of the ring are welded, as well as that the ring is welded to the rod.

Another heat is taken and the head is dressed more nearly to form with the hammer, and the bolt is placed in the heading tool or the swage block to bring the under side and the top of the head roughly to plane surfaces. The head is then laid in the groove of the swage block, and the swage used to form the sides of hexagonal head.

PRACTICAL EXAMPLES OF FORGING

53. Forging a Rocker-Arm From One Piece.—For this purpose, round stock is taken that is large enough in diameter to give, when flattened, the dimension at *a*, Fig. 58 (*a*),

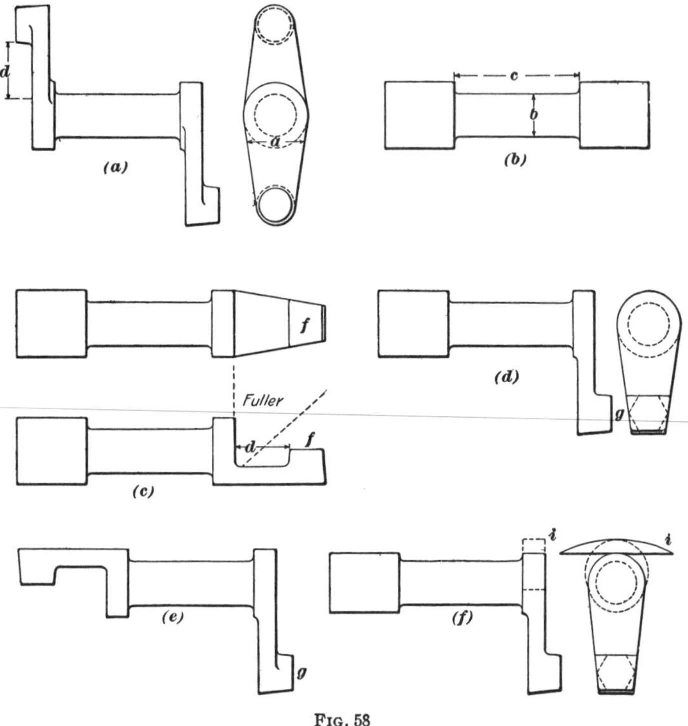

Fig. 58

and drawn to the form shown in Fig. 58 (*b*); this will require great care, for there is danger that the dimension *c* may be made too great, or, if this is right, that the dimension *b* may be too small. Enough of one end is flattened to form the arm, and drawn to the form shown in Fig. 58 (*c*). The dimension *d*, Fig. 58 (*c*), is made to correspond to *d*, Fig. 58 (*a*). In flattening this piece, the work is done with the hammer, the side toward which the stock is drawn being made as true and flat as possible from the shoulder to the end, and the recess at *d* formed by the use of the fuller; this leaves the stock *f* on the end, from which to form the boss. Next, the piece is clamped firmly near one shoulder and the flattened portion bent down, making the whole piece of the form shown in Fig. 58 (*d*). This may be done by clamping the piece between the hammer dies and driving down the arm with sledge hammers. The boss is rounded as shown at *g*, Fig. 58 (*e*), by first shaping it to the form shown by the dotted lines at *g*, Fig. 58 (*d*), and then rounding it to form the boss. The portion outside the shoulder on the other end of the piece is treated in the same manner, or both ends may be flattened and notched first, and then bent. Rocker-shafts are also forged by welding both arms to the shaft.

54. Forging a Rocker-Arm With Welded Shoulder. When it is not considered desirable to use stock that is large enough to form a shoulder of the required size, the shoulder should be made in the manner indicated in Fig. 58 (*f*). The rocker-arm is made from the stock at hand, leaving it too small at the shoulders and on the arms near the shoulders. A separate piece of stock is drawn to the form shown at *i*, Fig. 58 (*f*), and bent to fit closely around the shoulder that has been formed, as shown by the dotted lines. A welding heat is then taken in one shoulder, and that side is welded; this is repeated on the other side. After both shoulders have been treated in this way, the whole piece is gone over carefully and dressed to shape.

55. Locomotive Reverse Shaft.—The method of forging a locomotive reverse shaft varies in different shops, but a good way of doing it is shown in Figs. 59 and 60. The shaft is first heated at *a* where one of the arms is to be welded, and enlarged by upsetting, which is accomplished by swinging a heavy suspended steel ram *b*, Fig. 61, against its end, the shaft being supported in a special fixture or anvil *c*, Fig. 59, made for the purpose. Similar heats are taken at other points where arms are to be welded. The arms are previously forged, usually under a drop hammer. The end of each arm is split, and each end is drawn out, as shown at *e* and *f*, Fig. 60 (*b*). Fig. 60 (*c*) also shows some of the details of the form of the arms and shaft before welding. The small arm *a*, Fig. 60 (*a*), is first welded to the shaft, after which one of the link supporting

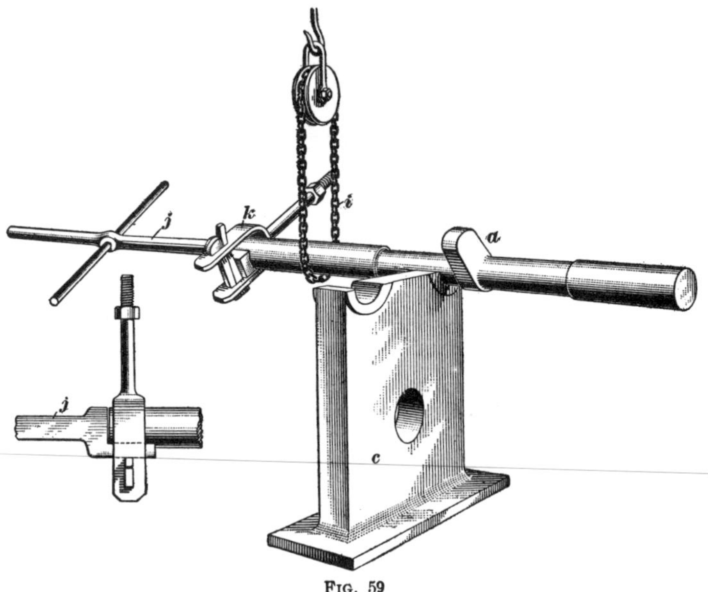

Fig. 59

arms *d* is welded on in the following manner: The shaft is heated in one fire and the end of the arm in another; when they are both at the proper heat, they are brought out, the shaft is dropped into the crotch of the special support *c*, and the arm placed on it. A few sharp blows on the upper end of the arm commence the weld at the center, and blows at *e* and *f*, Fig. 60 (*b*), complete it, a swage being used to finish the fillets about the end of the arm. The other arm *h* is then welded on in the same way.

The long arm *g* on the end of the shaft is sometimes made by first welding on a short piece, after which the shaft is taken to the machine shop for machining, and is then returned to the smith shop, and the remainder of this long arm welded on. The object of this method is to overcome the difficulty of turning the shaft in the lathe with the long arm on it.

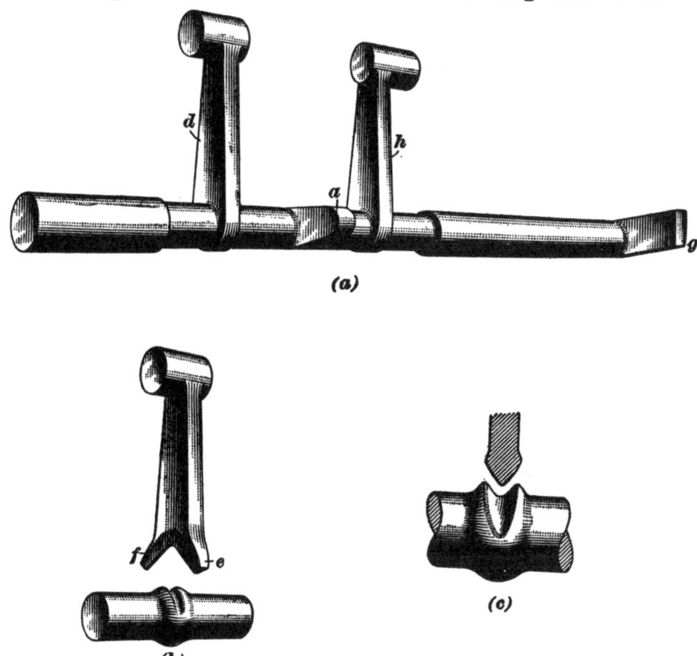

Fig. 60

During the welding the weight of the shaft is partially supported by the chain *i*, Fig. 59, hanging from a chain block on a swinging crane. The shaft is handled by the fixture *j*, which is fastened to it by means of a clamp *k* provided with a gib and key. The end of the clamp *k* has a thread and nut for the purpose of attaching weights to counterbalance the arms *d* and *h*. The main forge is located at *l*, Fig. 61. The forge in which the arms are heated is located at *m*. A cast-iron plate *n*, about 4 feet by 7½ feet in size, planed on the top and the edges, strongly ribbed on the bottom, and provided at one side with a pair of centers, adjustable lengthwise in a groove, is used to test the straightness of the shaft. There is a space of 3 or 4 feet between the fixture *c* and the plate *n*.

56. Locomotive Valve Yoke.—There are several methods of making a locomotive valve yoke. One of the

Fig. 61

best is to take a piece of square hammered iron, as shown by the dotted lines in Fig. 62, and draw one end as shown at *a*. The other end is split, opened out, and each end drawn out as shown at *b* and *c*, after which the two ends are split and bent down as shown at *d* and *e*. Another piece of iron is also drawn out to the proper size and length and bent as shown at *f*, with its ends properly scarfed for welding. First one side is welded and then the other, when it only remains to give the yoke the necessary finish. The clamp *g* is used to hold the parts in place while making the first weld at *e*.

57. Forging a Wrought-Iron Rudder Frame.—Many rudder frames of late years have been cast in open-hearth steel, in one piece, but owing to the possibility of hidden blow-holes, or invisible cracks in the corners, a wrought-iron frame is sometimes preferred. Fig. 63 shows such a frame in which it was necessary to make 19 welds, the location and order of which are shown by the figures, the dotted lines showing the character of each weld. Number *19* was made by welding in a diamond-shaped piece, or **glut,** which has the fiber of the iron lengthwise in the finished work.

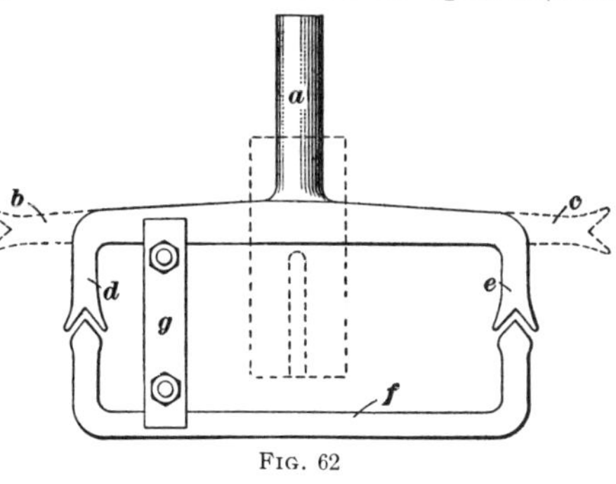

Fig. 62

The main piece, which in this case is 23 feet long, is shown at *a*. Eight inches of the upper end is square, below which

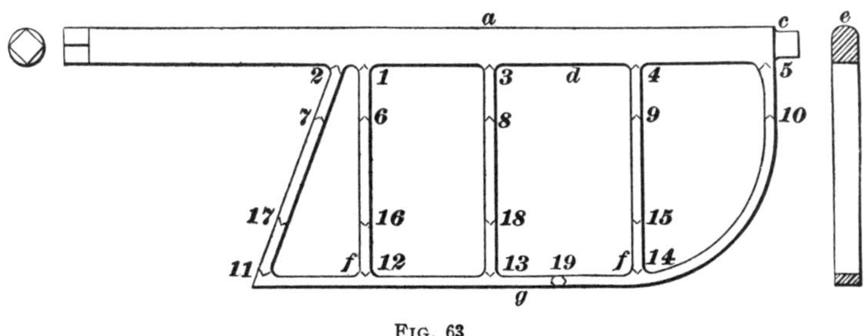

Fig. 63

it is turned 9 inches in diameter, a length of 6 feet. A pivot *c* is also turned at the lower end. The part of the frame *d* to which the arms are welded is square on that side and half round on the back, as shown in section at *e*. The arms, where they are joined to *d*, are from 3 to 4 inches by

$9\frac{1}{4}$ inches. At the outer end *f* they are 3 inches by $9\frac{1}{4}$ inches, and the part of the frame at *g* is the same size. Most of the welds are **V**-shaped, or cleft welds, but occasionally it is found advisable to make use of a double-cleft weld into which a diamond-shaped piece is welded. The most of the welding is done without taking the frame out of the fire. The frame, having been laid on a flat topped forge, is temporarily enclosed in firebrick at the point to be welded; the fire is then built under and around the point, the top of the brick-work being covered with several sections made up of an iron frame filled with firebrick and provided with a bail, or eye-bolt, for lifting the section to replenish the fuel or remove the work. Sometimes a chain fitted with a turnbuckle is so arranged on either side of the frame as to enable the parts that are to be welded to be drawn together. Two steel ramming bars are provided, each about 9 feet long and $1\frac{3}{4}$ inches in diameter, except at the working end, where they are $2\frac{1}{2}$ inches in diameter and slightly rounded. When the welding heat is reached, the turnbuckles are quickly tightened, the ramming bars introduced through either end of the furnace, and the scarf of the weld vigorously pounded down. The top covers of the furnace are then removed and three men with sledges finish the upper edge of the weld. The piece is then lifted out of the fire and placed on the anvil and the entire weld gone over with sledges, three men striking at the rate of about 36 blows each, or 108 blows per minute, on the work. Care is usually taken to have a little surplus stock at the weld, which is then trimmed off with a hot cutter.

58. Welding Pipe.—An open fire with an overhead hood is well adapted to pipe welding, which may be done in a forge fire in several ways. In the case of extra heavy iron or mild steel pipe welded together in lengths varying from two pipe lengths to 300 or 400 feet, as used for refrigerator coils and sometimes for steam coils for heating liquid, the pipe may be prepared by reaming it out at one end to a taper of about 60°, the other end being given an outside taper to match. This can be done on a turret machine or, with suitable dies, on a bolt cutter. For long lengths, a wooden trough or box, as long as the pipe, is usually provided. The ends of the pieces of pipe, with inside and outside taper, are placed in the fire and brought to a welding heat, using a little sand or other flux if the material requires it. The ends of the pipe are brought together in the fire, and two or three sharp blows are given on the cold end of one of the pipes by the helper, the smith meantime holding the other pipe. The weld is started by the blows on the end of the pipe, which is quickly drawn through the fire, bringing the weld into a bottom swage or on to an anvil located near the fire and directly under the pipe. The blacksmith applies a top swage, while the helper strikes light quick blows on the swage with a very light sledge hammer, the blacksmith turning the pipe meanwhile. The welding must be very quickly done, as pipe cools more quickly than solid iron. A few passes of a coarse file will remove the scale, and the pipe is then moved endwise in the trough for the next weld.

59. Welding Boiler Tubes.—Boiler tubes that have been burned or worn at one end may sometimes be repaired by cutting off from 4 to 6 inches of the defective ends and piecing them out by welding on new ends. Boiler tubes being generally made of good material, but thin, are not countersunk and tapered, but are heated at the end, one end being slightly enlarged on the horn of the anvil or on a tapered mandrel, and the end of the other piece being slightly tapered by swaging down. After the entire set of tubes, or at least a large number of them, and the short pieces have been thus prepared, the welding is proceeded with by putting them into the fire side by side, and bringing them quickly to the welding heat, rotating each in the meantime. The smith then takes the tube, and the helper the short piece, to the anvil, where they are put together, driven endwise, and swaged quickly to complete the weld.